Widows - Our Words and Ways

Widows - Our Words and Ways

A Collection of Personal Stories

BARBARA KRETCHMAR

MILL CITY PRESS

Mill City Press
2301 Lucien Way #415
Maitland, FL 32751
407.339.4217
www.millcitypress.net

Front Cover Design: Toby Meyer

Printed in the United States of America

ISBN-13: 9781545661062

My Dearest Ed,

**I will always love and respect you.
The world needs more Ed Kretchmars.**

PRAISE FOR
WIDOWS – OUR WORDS AND WAYS

"An inspiring book on a heart wrenching subject: Twenty-five widows speak for themselves, offering surprising comfort and unique survival strategies that only those who have been there could be wise enough to conceive."

Judith Sills, Ph.D., Psychologist, Author of the #1 *New York Times* best-seller *Excess Baggage*, Contributor to *The Today Show*, *Psychology Today*, past regular guest on *The Oprah Winfrey Show*.

"I know all too well the subject of this book. If only it had existed at the time of my loss. Yet, even now, this book has given much to me. In these pages, I hear the voices of women from all walks of life, united in the sharing of yesterday's loss and tomorrow's hope. More than consolation, *Widows – Our Words and Ways*, offers an outreached hand."

Linda Richardson, *New York Times* bestselling Author and Founder of Richardson, an International Sales Performance Company.

"Widow is a legal and demographic term that defines something that has happened. It tells us nothing of what the women experience and how they write the ongoing chapters of their lives. This collection of memories describes a wide spectrum of emotions, challenges and successes in a very compelling way."

Ann Rosen Spector, Ph.D., Clinical Psychologist, Columnist at *philly.com,* Contributor to *The Philadelphia Inquirer, Daily News.*

CONTENTS

INTRODUCTION .... **xv**

NARRATIVES

1 ~ Finding a Purpose — Laurada Byers **1**
*"I thought I had two or three choices: I could be a drunk in
the gutter, I could be angry and pull the covers over me, or
I could use Russell's death in some positive way.... I had to
find a purpose."*

2 ~ The Grief Spot — April H. **9**
*"The grief came from the core, in the center of the gut. It was
there for a long time—it was indescribable, a physical pain.
If you took an X-ray, you would be able to see the grief spot."*

3 ~ A Mind Game — Vicky A. **17**
*"Training for and participating in triathlons has helped me
more than anything else. ... Training makes everything better.
Triathlons are a mind game. I realized that if I can do this, I
can move forward."*

4 ~ Sometimes It's Good to Be Alone — Annie S. **25**
*"I believe a widow should think highly of herself as a human
being and should ask herself what will give her pleasure,
what she wants to do with the rest of her life. Yes, there
will be the times that you are alone. Sometimes it's good to
be alone."*

5 ~ The Hole in My Heart — Grace N. 33

"Not long ago, someone asked me if I was happy. I can't be happy as I once was because the hole in my heart is irreparable, but I can be content; I can be involved in meaningful business and social activities, and always be there for my son."

6 ~ Putting One Foot in Front of the Other Became My Mantra — Barbara Kretchmar 41

"No one emotion can describe my anguish, my anger, grief, sadness, fear, or loneliness. No one emotion because all these emotions were simultaneously riding high."

7 ~ I Was and Am Most Fortunate — Buntzie Churchill 51

"...I didn't know anything about our finances. I didn't even know where the safe deposit box was or what insurance policies there were...and most importantly, where the tuition money was hiding."

8 ~ How Was I Going to Spend the Rest of My Life? —Marilyn S. 57

"I was at a business dinner in New York City when I got the phone call that Warren had died....I was so relieved. It was over. He had been so sick, but now he was at peace. A huge burden had been lifted, and I was so happy for him."

9 ~ A Guiding Light — Sister Marcy 65

"There's a roadmap for everybody's life....Within each of us, there is a shining star, a guiding light, and if we just keep our focus and push towards that, we will find that we are more than we think we are."

10 ~ Do You! — Shannon McAuliffe 73

"But I decided that whatever I felt I needed to do, I would do. It didn't matter what anybody else thought. My motto was 'Do you!' I believe it's okay to be a little self-centered."

Contents

**11 ~ I Wasn't Afraid of Raising a Child Alone
— Carol Iamurri** **85**
"*Interestingly, in spite of Donny's death at 21, I never thought
of my own mortality or its consequences for my daughter.*"

**12 ~ If You're Here, Give Me a Sign
— Benita Leitner** **93**
"*Being Orthodox helped my grieving process. . . . To honor Scott,
I needed to be good and thankful for all the blessings in my life,
to go on for both of us and live a happy and positive life.*"

**13 ~ I Was Shocked ... Shocked That I Was
No Longer a Mrs. — Rita B.** **101**
"*After my husband's death, I had to transition quickly from
being a child to a grownup.... I had now inherited many
responsibilities.*"

14 ~ The Cubbyholes of Life — Maria D. **107**
"*To help with the grieving process, I came to visualize my life
in cubbyholes. Carlos' death was in one of the cubbyholes.
Sometimes it was as if I would take something out of that
cubbyhole, let myself think about it and cry, and then I would
put it back in.*"

**15 ~ I Was Scared That I'd Never Feel Joy Again
— Rochelle Toner** **115**
"*I think the grieving process is probably the same for a homosexual couple as it is for a heterosexual one, but the grieving
process might have been more difficult for me in a more
restricted atmosphere, in a different geography, if I had been
forced to live a more closeted life.*"

16 ~ The Shape of Grief — Tammy Banks **123**
"*It wasn't until years later that I found out that Zeke had
missed so many days of school not because he'd been sick
but because he'd been frightened of coming home from
school and finding me suddenly gone, just like his dad.*"

17 ~ The Terrible Problem of Loneliness — Patricia Goodman **129**
"His suicide was an escape from Alzheimer's and an act of compassion for us."

18 ~ Finding My Spark — Susan Gross **135**
"You have to cry, scream, punch pillows—you have to let it out, or you will crash. You can't program every single day so you don't have a moment to think. I needed to lie in bed a long time before I found my spark but I did find it."

19 ~ Women Mourn, Men Replace — Debby G. **141**
"We live in a couples' world, and that's the worst. People forget about you; it doesn't mean they don't like you, it's just that they forget about you."

20 ~ The Long, Winding Process of Grief — Sandy M. **147**
"I thought grief was something I could work through, like a college class. And, if I worked hard enough, maybe I could get over the grief before the baby came. Now I realize that grief is a long, winding process and we have minimal control over how quickly we process and heal."

21 ~ The Caregiver — Nora H. **157**
"He had been sick for 33 years and his death was a relief.... I never went through a period of sadness or grief.... I loved Tod very much but the years he had been ill had also taken a toll on me."

22 ~ A Guiding Spirit — Samisa S. **163**
"...right after my husband's death, I didn't believe in God anymore. I didn't want to have anything to do with Him. But now I understand that things happen for a reason."

23 ~ A Pretty Tough Lady — Liz R. 173
*"Grieve? I had no time to grieve; I had no time to breathe.
I had to be able to emotionally and financially support
my family."*

24 ~ A Dream of Polished Bronze — Wendy M........ 181
*"Seeing David in that dream changed things for me.... After
the dream, I did start dating and didn't feel guilty about
dating. I had felt numb for so long; I wanted to feel alive
again. I knew it's what David would have wanted."*

25 ~ Linda M. — It Will Get Easier 187
*"After Matt died, I was angry at God for a long time. I felt like
I was the first single parent that this had happened to. Why
had this happened to me?"*

ACKNOWLEDGMENTS 195

INTRODUCTION

I became a widow on March 6, 1990—a young widow with two small sons who were my only immediate family members. I needed emotional support. My friends and my colleagues at Scott Paper Company were there for me and I went for psychological counseling. I also thought it would be beneficial for me to connect with a bereavement group for younger widowed women who I believed could especially relate to my grief, but I couldn't find one. That continued to gnaw at me and was an impetus for writing this book.

Other than a few weeks off for marriage and childbirth, I practiced law continuously from 1967 until I retired in 2016. I then decided it was the appropriate time to couple my long-held ambition to write with my desire to help widows by writing a book in which a grieving widow, whoever she may be, could find one or more individuals or circumstances she could relate to and find some nuggets of wisdom to help her move forward with her life. This book is a personal recounting of the individual experiences of various widows, including my own. It is not intended as an instruction manual for widows. It is intended to be helpful and inspirational to grieving widows of different ages from diverse ethnic, racial, religious, educational and economic backgrounds, and for widows with or without children. It is also meant to offer support to women who become widowed under various circumstances—for example, whether a husband died suddenly or after a prolonged illness.

Becoming a bride, a wife, or a mother are joyous occasions; becoming a widow is not one. It's a painful, frightening and lonely circumstance. The Census Bureau has estimated that over one million women became widows in the United States in 2015 and the number of widows is seemingly increasing each year. Most women find themselves emotionally unprepared to deal with becoming a widow. As these stories attest, the grieving process often enables women to lead fulfilling lives after the death of their spouses, even though it may not be the life they had known before. The women in this book are all victims and survivors of widowhood. They are all everyday "wonder women," although most wondered how they would get through it. As they will tell you in these pages, it usually takes time, tears and thought.

I am not a psychiatrist, psychologist or therapist. I wrote this book because I am a widow who, like the other widows in this volume, experienced and survived the grieving process. This book is not a clinical manual on the best path a widow should follow to find her way through grief or at what speed. Nor is it one woman's account of the ordeals she endured during the initiation rites of becoming a member of a sorority she never pledged. Just as each of us is a different person, so is each widow unique. Regardless of who she is and the circumstances of her spouse's death, each widow shares certain commonalities in the challenges she has had to face: confronting the death of her spouse, experiencing the excruciating pain of grief, getting out from under the bedcovers and getting through each day and night, understanding and dealing with the changed realities of her life, learning how to navigate as a single person through a couples' world, and establishing a new life while attending to her family's and her own important needs. There is no one right answer, no one correct time frame.

This book is a collection of very human narratives of a broad spectrum of women, each of whom was widowed for at least two years at the time she was interviewed. As I mentioned earlier, the women are of various ages with diverse ethnic, racial, religious, educational and economic backgrounds; they became widows under different circumstances, and their personal histories and situations vary. The book is intended to speak to the new and not so new widow whoever she might be, who is feeling alone, bereft or sad and who is seeking to discover other widows whose experiences and emotions she can relate to; my wish is that reading these pages will make her feel less desolate. My hope is that these narratives will provide comfort and inspiration to her, as well as to other grieving widows, so that she might find a path through her grief.

In the following narratives, you will get to know a wide range of widows who have elected to share the intimacies of their lives, their pain and journey so that they may be of help to other widows. Each has survived it in her own way by finding her own sources of support and resources to move forward with her life. Many of the women have chosen to be identified by their real names, others desire more privacy and prefer the use of pseudonyms. When a narrator is identified by a first name and an initial, it is because she wishes to remain anonymous.

Each of these women is special with an inspiring story to tell. You will meet Carol, widowed at 21 and four months pregnant when her young, Good Samaritan husband was killed while breaking up a fight in an Army barracks as he awaited deployment to Vietnam. Just as Carol had to cope with raising a fatherless daughter, Sandy is now doing the same. She was 32 and three months pregnant when her husband died in 2012 under unclear circumstances while they were living in Africa. You will applaud Annie, who celebrated her 90th birthday in 2016. Twice widowed while in her sixties, she has since been involved in other longstanding relationships and gets up every morning thanking God for giving her another day. You will get to know women whose husbands committed suicide and learn how they grew from the experience. One of these women, Patricia, in her mid-sixties when confronted with her husband's suicide, found a new life as a poet, rediscovered her love of music and now sings both in a chorus and as a soloist. You will meet Laurada, whose prominent husband was murdered in front of her when they stopped to buy ice cream one Saturday evening at a local convenience store. She decided that rather than becoming "a drunk in the gutter," she would use his death in a positive way and founded a charter school. Sister Marcy's husband was also murdered, by a robber on a New York City street, leaving her with two young children. Unable to deal with her and her children's grief, she became a cocaine addict for four years until she fortuitously attended a church service that put her on the path to religious studies, to serving God and opening ministries in countries all over the world. While religion was a source of support to some widows of various faiths, whether Christian, Jewish, or Hindu, some non-religious widows sought or found comfort in other sources for an explanation of the enigma of death. A chance encounter with a medium changed one widow's views on the afterlife and helped her through her grief. Psychological counseling or therapy also helped a number of widows. We will meet widows who, while still grieving for their husbands, began socializing within days of the death, some who remarried a few years later and others who elected not to date or remarry. While grief was the common denominator among all these women, each eventually realized she had to deal with her grief in a constructive manner that worked best for her and allowed her to move forward.

You can open this book to any page and find stories that, while especially relevant to certain categories of widows, also speak to all widows, and that offer wisdom germane to any grieving widow. These narratives are incisively real, thought-provoking and elegant. The stories of the gracious and wonderful widows in this book who so very generously and altruistically shared their own personal and painful passage through widowhood will resonate with and provide solace, encouragement and inspiration to grieving widows seeking their own path through their grief to a better day ahead.

A close friend once asked whether I had become depressed after speaking with so many widows. I replied that at no point during these interviews had I become depressed; to the contrary, I came away with a feeling of awe, of reverence for the resilience of the women whose stories appear in this book. I am very grateful to them for their trust in me, for sharing the intimacies of their lives as well as for taking the time to be interviewed, to review the various drafts of the narratives I wrote and to comment or correct the narratives as needed.

The interviews were conducted between March 2016 and late 2017 either in person or over the telephone, depending on geographic proximity and the preference of the interviewee. The narratives express the interviewee's experiences, feelings and thoughts as of the time of her interview. I hope my recounting of their stories does them justice.

~1~

Laurada Byers — Finding a Purpose

"I thought I had two or three choices: I could be a drunk in the gutter, I could be angry and pull the covers over me, or I could use Russell's death in some positive way. I decided that his death had been so awful that I just couldn't be angry and let it go at that."

Laurada Byers, founder and Chair of the Byerschool Foundation, was 51 when her husband, Russell Byers, 59, was stabbed to death in front of her in 1999. He had been an influential columnist at the *Philadelphia Daily News* who was passionate about government, urban issues and improving Philadelphia.

*A*s we were returning home from a Saturday night party, Russell and I stopped at a local Chestnut Hill convenience store to purchase ice cream. As we walked back to the car, a young man emerged from the bushes and pointed a gun at Russell's head. It looked almost like a cartoon, as Russell was 6'6" and his assailant was 5' 2". The man never asked Russell for his wallet, he just said, "Give me your keys." Russell, concerned about the gun, tried to move him away from the car and me. We had no idea that this 19-year-old also had a knife until he stabbed Russell in the heart. Bleeding, he staggered into the store while I yelled, "Help him!" I was giving him CPR when a policeman pulled me off, saying, "Lady, what are you doing? He's dead." During the preceding violence, I had an out-of-body experience—for 15 seconds, I just wasn't there.

I was in shock and freezing cold. The police drove me home and I phoned my stepchildren, Alison and Russell, Jr. After changing out of my blood-soaked clothes, I went with the police to the Round House in Center City to answer their questions. At the Round House, I called Zach Stalberg, editor of the *Daily News*, to tell him of Russell's death, saying, "Here's a scoop for you." Zach drove me home, made phone calls and stayed overnight at the house. Still freezing and in shock, I went into a cleaning frenzy: I was thinking about all the people who would be over at the house the next day. Zach called my friend, Caroline Stewart Lacey, a former *Daily News* reporter who had worked with Russell. She came over at 6:00 A.M. and other people started coming over about 7:30. Alison and Russell Jr., both married and in their 30's, arrived with their dogs by noon. I remember lots of dogs running around—their dogs, our dogs.

We organized the memorial service that was held the following Wednesday at the Friends Meeting House in Center City. Although Russell was Catholic and I was Episcopalian, we both thought Quaker meeting services were very free-flowing, reflective and spiritual. Over a thousand people attended. A number of people had been asked to speak but some of the most remarkable tributes to Russell were from people we didn't know. The service was very beautiful and comforting. I think that people really appreciated coming together to reflect, especially given what had happened. The memorial service is a memory I hold dear. Going through the ritual of the memorial service was very cathartic: I think that's why we have these rituals.

I do believe in God but I'm a spiritual rather than a religious person. I struggled and tried to understand why this had happened to me. Did it have a purpose? Did I have a purpose? I questioned a friend, a former monk and later a successful businessman: is there free will or is there predestination? He said, "Life is very random, it's random that Russell got murdered. What you decide to do afterwards, Laurada, is a function of who you are; it has nothing to do with religion or God." I thought I had two or three choices: I could be a drunk in the gutter, I could be angry and pull the covers over me, or I could use Russell's death in some positive way. I decided that his death had been so awful that I just couldn't be angry and let it go at that, I had to find a purpose.

Within three months, I had begun discussing with family and friends how to honor Russell's life. As Russell had written about politics, urban affairs, and charter schools, it was very logical for me to do something connected to charter schools—even though my former careers in real estate, manufacturing stuffed animals and marketing had nothing to do with education. I used to joke that "Russell wrote about it, but I had to do something about it." We formed a committee to create a charter school; in my absence, the committee decided I should be its CEO. Because charter schools are supposed to be innovative change agents, I visited 36 different kinds of schools.

I found one model called Expeditionary Learning Outward Bound that not only appealed to me; I thought it would have appealed to Russell as well. Out of 27 charter schools applying for approval, ours, the Russell Byers Charter School, was one of three chosen. Establishing the school was my major source of distraction in the period following Russell's death; starting a charter school is not easy and it kept me busy and focused. Focusing was especially difficult because in addition to recovering from Russell's death, I was suffering from post-traumatic stress disorder (PTSD). I couldn't read, watch TV or concentrate. Because I had no short-term memory, my friend Caroline went with me to all the meetings concerning the school. She took notes and remembered all that had occurred. Although I could perform just fine during the meetings, once out of the meeting I had no recollection of what had happened, what the next steps were. Caroline gave up seven years of her life helping me to ensure that the school was a success.

Because I didn't know how I was supposed to behave as a widow, I asked my friend Judy von Seldeneck to organize a dinner for me each week with a different widow. I wanted women who would be diverse in age and who had been widowed under diverse circumstances; the idea was that they would tell me what I could expect my life to be like, what would upset me, what would make me crazy. Judy arranged these dinners and I had some really interesting and very helpful conversations. There were certain consistent themes and learning: everyone will be very solicitous for the first couple months, then you'll fall off the radar; save some of your friends for later because although you will be very busy at first, you'll be forgotten later; be careful because at first, you can get very tired or drink more than usual as everyone is taking you out to dinner. One thing I absolutely knew: I had to keep up my daily exercise regimen, which had always been extremely important to me.

Although the school kept me busy, it wasn't an aid to me in the grieving process because for a couple of years after Russell's death I was afraid to grieve. I was afraid I would start crying and never stop—and then what? I was in therapy for a couple of years. I appeared to be normal on the surface, but I had nightmares for years. Subconsciously I was grieving, but consciously, I didn't know it. I'm not certain I'm grieving now. I didn't find those five stages of grieving to be helpful. In addition to grieving, I had the enormous problem of PTSD to cope with. Because PTSD is a physical condition of the brain, talk-therapy isn't helpful. It took ten years to figure out a proper method to deal with my PTSD.

I decided to visit Russell's murderer in jail. Allison, a clinical therapist, warned that it would just stir up all the bad memories and exacerbate my PTSD, but I decided to do it for two reasons. First, I wanted to get this boogeyman out of my life. Secondly, I wanted to talk to him to see what I could learn that I could bring back to the school. It was extremely difficult to get the necessary approval for Caroline and me to visit him and it took three years to set the meeting up. We were not allowed to bring in anything other than the one sheet of paper on which I had written the questions I wanted to ask him. At the start of the interview, he asked if I was mad at him. Not wanting to cede any power to him, I said, "No, I'm not mad at you. I'm completely indifferent to you. You're like a bug to me. My children are mad at you, but I'm not." The two hour visit with him was informative. On getting out of reform school, he needed money so he decided to hijack a car. Then, he decided to make it his career. He told me what he had believed to be true: "Yes, I'm a career criminal. If I get caught, I'll only go to jail for five years." He was furious that he had gotten a sentence of life with no parole for his attempted carjacking and murder of Russell. He had appealed his sentence to no avail, claiming that he had been represented by ineffective counsel because his lawyer had worn boat shoes to court. He had no remorse for what he had done—and that was absolutely terrifying to me. It disturbed me to think that we could be producing career criminals. Although the visit didn't provide me with closure and it exacerbated my PTSD, it was instructive. I realized that although our schools teach English, math, and science, until we've dealt with instilling character, we have not done our job. Because of that visit, character development is a very important issue at our school.

There were other issues I faced as a widow. The most difficult was being responsible for one's own life when you're used to sharing a life. There's also the loneliness, the isolation. Right after Russell's death, people would literally cross the street to avoid me. Many people can't deal with death, especially death in these circumstances. I wasn't disappointed in these people; I would probably have behaved in the same way. The house that we had lived in for 17 years was no longer a sanctuary for me. Approximately three years after Russell's death, I made the decision to move and found a perfect apartment in the City.

For the first few years after Russell's death, I was not part of any world. My life consisted of establishing the school. (Ironically, the school opened on September 11, 2001.) During that time, I sometimes found myself avoiding people. I had no energy left at night for a social life. I had to go to fundraising events for the school. I would go to a cocktail party, but then I would bolt—I didn't have the patience for dinner, I just had to get out of there. I still don't like crowds.

About three years after Russell's death, I started dating men that friends introduced me to. I was in a long-term relationship with a lovely, older gentleman—a wonderful companion—that I ended a few years ago when I wasn't able to provide him with the attention his medical condition required. Today, I'm receptive to dating but I'm not expecting to find the love of my life. Actually, I wonder if Russell would fall in love with me if he met me now. He was the bigger-than-life person, and I was the person behind the scenes who made things work. I'm no longer that person behind the scenes. It was hard transitioning from a private person to a public person. I find that now I'm much less patient, much less accommodating—I've got things to do.

Since Russell's death, I have learned that life goes on. I don't think anger is productive; instead, I focus on feeling

7

blessed by the experiences I've had, the people I've met and the opportunity to lead the life I've had both with and without Russell. That's why I compiled two books of blessings. I firmly believe there are no coincidences in life and that things happen for a reason. Ultimately, we are responsible for our lives and the sooner we recognize that and act accordingly, the happier we'll be.

~ 2 ~

April H. – The Grief Spot

"The grief came from the core, in the center of the gut. It was there for a long time—it was indescribable, a physical pain. If you took an X-ray, you would be able to see the grief spot."

April was 36 when her husband, 41, died of a heart attack in 2003, leaving her with a daughter, five, and a son, three. She is a program coordinator at a special education preschool and had been working towards her Ph.D. in Developmental Psychology when her husband died.

*M*y husband of 11 years was on his way back home to New York when he collapsed in my parents' driveway in New Jersey in 2003. He was rushed to the hospital but he could not be resuscitated. That night I had to start making decisions. I received a call from an organ donor organization asking me to donate his long bones and his eyes. I agreed to donate his bones but not his eyes. We had planned an open casket at the wake and I didn't want my children to see their father looking different than when he did when he was alive. I did request an autopsy for my children's sake so I could learn of any genetic issues they might inherit from their father.

The following morning I had to tell my children that their father was dead. I told them his heart had stopped working, and although the doctors had done their best to get it working again, they could not and he had died. Although my parents were present, I thought it best to tell the children alone, just by myself. I held them as they cried and I did my best to comfort them. At one point, my three-year-old son, who is a concrete thinker, asked, "Can we just go to the store and get a new dad?" Afterwards, he kept asking me whether his father would be coming back. Actually, having to tell him repeatedly that his father was not coming back helped me process the finality of my husband's death.

After my husband's death, it was all about the children. I was not only a single parent—I was a solo parent. They were the reason I got out of bed. They were the push, the impetus, to get through the quicksand. I think my professional background was helpful in guiding both the children and me through the grieving process. Interestingly, I think that because of my background, I moved through the grieving process for a long time at two levels: I was objectively observing it as a third person and I was also personally experiencing it. It was important to me that my children understand the emotionality of their father's death so they could feel all the things they needed to feel. I didn't want them to worry about how sad I was or they were or about how sad all the people they loved were too.

I remember having one immediate thought that was directed to my husband, "Why do I have to go through this without you? You're my best friend, so who do I turn to at a time like this but my best friend? And yet it's you I'm grieving." But I was fortunate in that I had a strong immediate support group of close family and friends who lived nearby and who were perceptive in taking cues, and understanding and respecting when we needed to be by ourselves.

I believe in an afterlife. I knew that my husband was gone, but it wasn't like that was that—I believed I would see him again. I was raised as a Catholic and our children were being raised as Catholics, so after his death I went to church, I went to Mass. I knew that the ritual and prayer of the Mass would *eventually* be a source of comfort to me. But returning to church as this newly shaped family right after his death seemed to mark his absence in a profound way for me—not unlike so many other things I needed to learn to do without him. He was just missing.

Shortly after my husband's death, I went to a therapist who recommended a support group, but I wasn't yet ready. I think one has to be really brave to be in front of a big group, and I needed to be dealing with my grief by myself. But in September the children and I joined Caring Circle, a most wonderful support group for the family. A Caring Circle social worker came to the house to talk with us before we went to the first bi-weekly session, so that she would be a familiar face when we walked in. After the families met all together in a group, the children were separated by age and played together while I met with other mothers. We all then gathered together again at the end of the session. We attended the Caring Circle sessions for about a year.

It was an excellent experience for the kids; they met and played with other children who had also lost a parent. I remember that shortly after we started attending, my daughter said, "Mom, I just met a boy whose Dad also died." It normalized things for my kids; they met other children who had experienced what they had. It was a beginning for them.

Grief is tough. First, I grieved for my children, and then I grieved for myself. Sometimes I just needed space to cry by myself. The grief came from the core, in the center of the gut. It was there for a long time — it was indescribable, a physical pain. If you took an X-ray, you would be able to see the grief spot. I sometimes think of the grieving process as being at boot camp. Imagine what it's like at first: you have to carry an 80-pound pack on your back and you can't walk with it. You can't even get off the floor because it feels so heavy. That's what grief feels like. But you carry it and with time you learn to live with it and it's not so heavy. I also think of it like waves: the waves come quickly, and then they die down; then a big one comes along and you're never prepared for it. It may be the day after Christmas, the day after Father's Day, or whenever. The wave is always there, it's waiting for you.

My job is to keep my children happy: their father's death is going to affect them for the rest of their lives. I've been very open about making sure I and the children got psychological help when we needed it. "I need help; it's okay for you to need help." They were never resistant. I felt especially sorry for my son, who never had any real memories of his father and didn't have a father to pattern himself after. Grief is one thing — and I had close friends and family — but you also have to deal with loneliness after a spouse's death. It was tough and a big problem. Ultimately, I had to learn how to make decisions, big and small, by myself. And it's been tough for me to face the different, significant milestones in my kids' lives that my husband, their father, is missing.

The first year is tough. It's a year of first everythings — holidays, vacations. And I had to learn how to be by myself, how to take care of the house, how to be father and mother. When my husband died I immediately stopped pursuing my Ph.D. There was no time for that, as I was busy parenting and working. By nature I tend to be a fixer and caregiver, so I quickly went into that mode. It made me functional, but I also let a piece of myself slip away. A friend said, "I know April is in there somewhere." I had to learn how to be happy again, how to take care of myself. I had put myself on the backburner, and I didn't make time for interests or pursuits outside of my kids. It took me a long time to find my way back and I still struggle with it. At first, I spent time only with my children. I had to make sure that nothing bad would happen, and that meant I didn't go out and do anything for myself—even to go by myself to a friend's house—because maybe that's when bad things would happen. Not going out to do things for myself was my way of exercising emotional control that bad things wouldn't happen. It was okay if my kids went to a friend's house, but I was afraid that bad things would happen if I went somewhere without my children – I just couldn't leave anything up to chance. I had to overcome the fear that I could be good to myself without bad things happening to my children. A therapist had to teach me to take baby steps and see that I could be good to myself without bad things happening to my kids. Thirteen years later, I still have not gotten on an airplane by myself or with anyone other than my children.

I was afraid I would die and then I couldn't be there for my children, and they had the same fear. That fear interfered with my quality of life and my ability to navigate this new world I found us in. Because people do die, I didn't want to say that I would always be there for them, but I did try to reassure them. I wore my seatbelt in the car, and I went to the doctor regularly so I could tell my kids I was healthy.

After my husband died, I had to learn how to be happy again as a woman – but in a new way. I'm different now because of my loss, so I have to find my happiness in a different way. It's a gradual process. One thing I did—about a year after my husband's death, I decided to paint the interior walls of my house. They'd always been white, but I wanted to paint them a different color, to fill in and redefine the space. I also bought new living room furniture. Maybe doing the painting and redefining my space was a way of taking control, of redefining my new life.

I never felt like the odd woman out with my closest friends, but after a year or two, I looked around and saw friends who were couples going on with their lives and I wasn't included. I kind of felt hurt by that but I also knew that I probably wouldn't have been all that comfortable in their company. It also made me sad because I realized that if my husband were still alive, we would be doing the same things as those couples.

About four years after my husband had died, I decided to start dating. Some of my friends knew me when my husband was alive as part of a couple and others first met me and knew me as a widow. I started meeting the latter group of women when the children went to school and I had lived for a longer time in the community. These women never knew me as a wife, so they hadn't seen me go through the grief. I think they were more honest with me—they saw me for who I was now. A few told me that they thought it was time for me to date, that I was ready, and I agreed. I knew that I hadn't been feeling good when I walked into a room, that I felt like I had a Scarlet W on my chest. I also knew that there was more to me than being a widow. So I thought, "Yes, I need a grownup to talk to at the end of the day."

I met the first man I dated online. I think I kept him at emotional arm's length, but we dated on and off for years. At first, I kept my dating to myself. I was always very conservative and mindful about allowing any man into my home who didn't pass muster. Still, it was difficult for my daughter to accept my interest in any man other than her father.

I'm proud of myself, how I've grown. People compliment me on how well I have raised my children. I don't always integrate it, but then I think, "Oh my God, I did this, I really did it. I've come a long way and grown a lot." Because of my husband's death, I'm a different woman than the one my husband married. I sometimes wonder if he would still love me as I am now. I think so. My experiences after his death have changed me but I'm still me at the core.

Personally, I think you should keep a little of the sadness with you, a little bit of the love. You love him, you'll always miss him. If you love someone, there's never enough time. Even if your husband is 89 when he dies, it's still sad. It's now 14 years later and I still want my husband back, but maybe it would be different if I were to find another partner for life. There's no roadmap, no guidebook. Just listen to yourself.

~ 3 ~

Vicky A. — A Mind Game

*"Training for and participating in triathlons has
helped me more than anything else…Training
makes everything better. Triathlons are a mind game.
I realized that if I can do this, I can move forward."*

Vicky, a feisty business entrepreneur, was widowed in 2008 at 56 when her husband died after a nearly two-year struggle with prostate cancer. When he was diagnosed, their son, 21, was away at college, and their daughter, 17, was a senior in high school.

*K*en had been diagnosed in 2006 with a very aggressive form of prostate cancer that had metastasized to his bones. We had been married almost 30 years. Incidentally, I proposed to Ken two weeks after knowing him: he was kind, he was considerate, he was an architect, and the sex was good. Ken said he needed to know me for a year before we could get married and I agreed. Two weeks before the year was up, I reminded him of that; I said it would be fine if he didn't want to get married but I would be packing up and leaving town. Ken, who never cursed, said, "Oh, fuck. Let's get married." We were married four weeks later at City Hall in a non-religious ceremony.

When Ken was diagnosed, we were told that at best he had three years to live. First, he went through hormone therapy, then radiation, then chemotherapy, and then pain management. We went through all the complications of cancer. Dealing with the hospital's medical staff was a total nightmare that left me astounded and furious. I'll never forget one nurse practitioner: before there was even a prognosis on Ken's prostate cancer, she came into his hospital room and started questioning me about hospice care decisions. I asked her who she was, profanely told her what she could do with herself, said I never wanted to see her again and kicked her out of the room. There were plenty more idiots who I unfortunately had to deal with. I had instructed the doctors that Ken was dedicated to his career and no matter what they had to keep him working. Despite being tired, in pain and undergoing the various treatments, Ken worked for 18 of the 21 months that he was sick—until he developed cellulitis. I continued working throughout his illness.

Every marriage has phases: there's the beginning period, which is great, and then the middle period, the dark stage. Ken and I had been going through the dark stage for quite a while. Although I hadn't directly told him, I harbored very serious thoughts that I was going to leave him. I felt like my self-worth had been beaten up because of Ken's withdrawn attitude. He had poured all his concentration and energy into his work and he had little left for me and the kids. I couldn't take it anymore. But the minute he was diagnosed, all thoughts of leaving him went out the window, all the anger dissipated; I had been married to him for almost 30 years. We kind of rediscovered each other; a friend even commented that we looked cute together. When horrible things like that happen, you either fall apart or you don't. I decided I wasn't going to fall apart. Decisions have to be made and I decided to do the best I could.

After all the months of treatment, Ken fell down in the spring of 2008 and couldn't get up. Once he made it up, he could barely walk. He went into the hospital for five days, which was truly the beginning of the end. The doctors found a tumor pressing on his spine. They recommended surgery to remove the tumor and relieve the pressure. The man was dying, but he agreed. After a two-week post-operative period in the hospital, Ken was sent to a rehab center even though I wanted him home. After about two weeks, the rehab center called me and—this is brilliant—said it was discharging Ken because of his failure to progress: hello, the man was dying! While they were in the process of kicking him out of the rehab center and I was on the phone with the admin person, I received a separate call from the center that Ken had gone into cardiac distress and was being rushed back to the hospital.

I rushed to the hospital, where a friend was already waiting for me. The kids were in New York. I called them and told them they had to come home to say their goodbyes. At 3:00 A.M. that morning, I sent my friends and family home from the hospital and climbed into bed with Ken. It may sound like a cliché, but I said, "Sweetheart, if you want to go, it's okay,

I understand. We'll be okay." He hung on until the morning. Actually, the minute Ken died, I was in the hospital room with two good friends and we were bad-mouthing our husbands. I joked, "Well, he got tired of me bad mouthing him." There is no living without humor. After Ken died, I sent everyone out of the room and cried like I had never cried before. Then I talked to Ken, assuring him that all would be okay. I still periodically have conversations with him. The kids got to the hospital 15 minutes too late.

I am Jewish; Ken was not. Neither of us was religious. My children, Ken's brothers and I agreed on plans for his burial. When we first bought our home, Ken was into French biodynamic gardening. He would periodically collect his urine, dilute it and deposit it in the garden. After he was cremated, we scattered his ashes in the garden during a gathering of our friends and family. Ken, the architect, was into sustainability; he would have liked that his burial service didn't leave a carbon footprint.

My friends were my support group when Ken died—thank God for good friends. My parents were not a source of support, and I was angry at them. They flew in for the funeral and I arranged for them to stay in a hotel because I wanted to give my kids the freedom to express themselves without any one besides me being present—they were my first concern. But then my parents were upset because they felt we didn't need them, and they left in the middle of the burial service. They wanted my son to drive them to the airport. I told them to call a cab and didn't talk to them for six months.

I was tired, exhausted, but I went back to work a week after Ken died. I got in early before anyone else because I didn't want to talk to people. I didn't want people asking me questions, and I didn't want people feeling sorry for me.

The first three months after Ken died were a blur. Not only was I exhausted, I was sad, the kids were sad. My own life felt disjointed. At around the three-month mark, I said, "Okay, Ken, enough of this, you can come back now. Come home, come home." It was just hard: I was tired, tired of making decisions, and I couldn't imagine making decisions for the rest of my life without him. I went to a grief counselor at that time because I couldn't understand why Ken wasn't coming home, why he wasn't walking through the door.

I don't think I was rational for the first six months. I was functioning but I was in a fog, and I wasn't thinking. My status had changed—I was now a widow. I couldn't understand why my car insurance had gone up just because I was a widow.

I was very concerned about my kids. My son expressed his grief by getting kicked out of college for not doing his schoolwork. My daughter was angry at Ken for dying and because he had been distant, and she was angry at me because I was a little crazy. We really fought with each other; she thought I was angry with her, and I was afraid I was going to lose her. It took several years for us to rebuild a vocabulary where we could talk to each other and reconcile.

I was furious at Ken: he should have gone to the doctors earlier, our relationship should have been better during that middle stage of our marriage. I was probably angry at him for about a year. I was told that it was typical for me to react that way. It sounds surreal, but I had a birthday dream the first year after Ken died that was so real that I could touch Ken in his architect uniform of tweed jacket, black shirt with wooden buttons and chinos. I absolutely love James Bond movies and I am convinced that on my birthday, Ken came and took me to the new James Bond movie.

During that first three months after Ken died, we experienced what my daughter called "our 15 minutes of fame." People were inviting us to dinner because they knew we had experienced a loss and they felt they had to take care of us. It's not the first, second or third month that you need people around; it's month four, it's the following year that you need people to ask how you're doing, ask if you want to talk about it or invite you to dinner.

About a year after Ken died, my son trained for a marathon and tried to convince me to do the same. I'm a horrible athlete, but I decided I'd try doing a triathlon with him rather than a marathon—I thought it would be easier. It was a wonderful decision because training for and participating in triathlons has helped me more than anything else. We did our first triathlon in Chicago…what an experience. Training makes everything better. Triathlons are a mind game. I realized that if I can do this, I can move forward. I met new people, younger people. I still do triathlons, I'm still moving forward!

After Ken's death I began to feel like I was the third or fifth wheel. It wasn't something that happened all the time but it was disquieting when it did happen. People who knew you as a couple now know you for what you've gone through, and they see you now as a widow. But I wanted to be known as me. In 2014, after the economy and housing market had improved, I sold my house. I rented an apartment while I tried to figure out where I wanted to live. I was restless and wanted to make a change. The idea of moving to a completely new place was intriguing. I saw it as an adventure and as the opportunity to figure out who I was and who I wanted to be. I love the outdoors, so in 2015 I moved to a city in North Carolina's western Blue Ridge Mountains. I knew no one there but it's an area where Ken and I had taken our children camping. I bought a small house, made new friends and I became part of my neighborhood. I have also gotten involved in community activities, from human rights groups to Meetup groups to a knitting circle where I can drop in on a Saturday afternoon when I feel like knitting and chatting. I'm making a new life. People know I have children, and some know I am a widow. It's beginning to feel like home. Here, I can be known as me, and, it's also giving me the space to figure who I am and what's next for me.

I'm not interested in remarrying or living with someone. For a long time I had no interest in dating, but now I'm open to dating. I would like the companionship—I miss the physical companionship. I even tried online dating a couple of times, but it was a disaster.

I have some learning to offer: Don't do anything the first year, and make no financial decisions. Go with your grief. Ride the emotions—because they're there. You can't fight them. It took me three years, but some people come out of it earlier. Give yourself the time you need, but at some point you have to move forward—you can't go through life in a fog. I try to be there for my kids, my friends, and my parents. Life goes on, and you have to take care of yourself.

~ 4 ~

Annie S. — Sometimes It's Good to Be Alone

"I believe a widow should think highly of herself as a human being and should ask herself what will give her pleasure, what she wants to do with the rest of her life. Yes, there will be the times that you are alone. Sometimes it's good to be alone."

Annie, a former school teacher, was born in 1926. She does not believe in the concept of young or old. She was widowed twice and has been in a relationship for the last seven years.

I celebrated my 90th birthday in 2016, but age is just a state of mind to me and doesn't reflect how old I am. What I am is a very happy person and although I'm not a particularly religious person, I wake up every morning and thank God for another day.

I was married in 1946 at 19 when I was still in college; my husband, Ronnie, was 28, nine years older. We were married for 40 years and have three grown children. I was 60 when Ronnie died. Life had not always been easy while he and I were married. Although he was an accomplished professional, there were periods when he was unemployed and we had financial concerns. After Ronnie was diagnosed with colon cancer, we struggled with its many consequences during the last two and a half years of his life. When he was no longer able to go to his doctor's office, he had his treatments at home. It was a difficult time. Ronnie could not work, nor could he do much of anything. I taught elementary school and because we had no outside help, I rushed home at lunch to take care of him. He finally had to be admitted to the hospital. A few weeks after he was admitted, the hospital called to say that I should rush over because he was in a bad way. I raced to the hospital where I held Ronnie's hand, and said, "It's okay, I can take care of myself. I'll be okay. You can let go now." Then he died peacefully and I removed his wedding ring. There had been so much aggravation and stress in my life and now I knew that I faced the difficulty of being alone but not knowing how I was going to handle it. I hadn't thought about this before because I had been very busy working. It was work that had kept me going: I had a responsible teaching job that I not only loved but was also very financially important to us because of Ronnie's employment history. Because at one point Ronnie worked out of town during the week and only came home on weekends,

I soon became confident that could I live alone, manage the household and finances, and survive as a widow. I did once go to a bereavement group—just once. Everyone there, including me, just talked about their problems. I knew I had to work things out, to stand on my two feet or fall. I didn't see where this group was going to help me move forward. I didn't go again and I didn't look for another group. Emotional support? Sitting Shiva provided me some comfort as did the cantor and his wife. And I always found support from my children and grandchildren, with whom I spent a lot of time.

But right after Ronnie died my circle of couple friends shrank because I was no longer a couple—that was very hard. I found there were people who deserted me; some people I thought were my friends acted like they just didn't care. My bridge group just dropped me. They gave me no explanation, but they were all couples and I was a single. Couples didn't make me part of their world. About the only couples who really kept in touch were friends from a local environmental nature group that I had been involved with. I spent a lot of time with them. I was lonely after Ronnie's death but I knew that I had to be strong and take care of myself. I went on my first date about five or six months after Ronnie died. I never looked for someone to date—someone just popped up. My first date was a blind date with a man my eye doctor fixed me up with. I was so nervous because I felt like a dummy. Would I eat properly, what would I say? I felt uncomfortable on that date but after that date I had confidence in myself and only dated men who made me feel comfortable.

I didn't entertain any thoughts of remarrying after Ronnie's death. Then, through happenstance, I met Stuart. About 18 months after Ronnie died, I invited some of his friends to dinner, people I hadn't seen in a long time. The wife suggested I also invite Stuart, a college friend of Ronnie's whose wife had recently died. He was a lovely man, seven or eight years older than I, who lived in Westchester County. He played golf and tennis, loved the arts, had his own plane and was a down to earth guy. He hadn't been aware that Ronnie had died. We ended up having a lovely evening.

Two weeks later, Stuart asked me out to see an exhibit at the Metropolitan Museum of Art. After that, I spent all my weekends with him. Thinking back, I'm quite sure that while I was in the kitchen that first night, preparing dinner for Ronnie's friends and Stuart, I heard Stuart mention he had some blood problem, but I ignored it. After I started dating him, I never thought of him as a potentially ill man. It's not that I blocked it; it's that I loved him so much that I never thought about or paid any attention to his blood problem. He was so loving and caring, and that was so appealing to me. Stuart asked me to marry him and I agreed because I loved him so much.

We had a big, beautiful wedding, and Stuart died four months later. At 63, I was widowed again. When we got married, I sold my house and all of its contents and moved to Stuart's house. We lived there for about six weeks before we went on our honeymoon. When we were in Paris, Stuart became ill, and we returned home. He was diagnosed with leukemia. After initially receiving treatment at a local hospital, we moved Stuart to a hospital in Manhattan for treatment. I was at the hospital with him all day until nighttime, and then stayed the night at a cousin's apartment. I only left Stuart to attend to matters in Westchester County on Sundays after his son's visits.

I was truly devastated when Stuart died. It was harder for me than when Ronnie died. Now I really needed help. I was living in a strange area in a strange house with nothing that was mine. At first, I didn't know what to do, where to go. I had no friends there and no one there knew me. I realized that I had to make a place for myself here and a new life, see what it was like, and then make decisions. What else was I going to do? I became active in the community. I started doing volunteer work at a hospital where I met a lovely woman for whom I cared very much and I spent a lot of time with her and her husband. They hold a special place in my heart. I found that people were very welcoming to me. I joined the tennis club where Stuart had been a member and found people to play with who were new to me. I joined a Great Books group. This time I didn't go to a bereavement group but I was fortunate to meet and become very good friends with a wonderful woman who counseled widows on a volunteer basis.

After two years, I felt I needed to move back to the area where I had previously lived. Once again, I had to make a new life for myself. I bought a coop apartment in a gated residential community in Queens that has tennis courts and an 18-hole golf course. I love where I live. Because I was in my 60's, it was hard at first to find a tennis group but I did. I took golf lessons and became an enthusiastic player. If I felt lonely when I first moved here, I would go down to the coffee shop, buy coffee and a paper and sit there and read—I met people that way.

I was fortunate that I was never without someone to date. Interesting men just kept turning up. I knew I didn't want to get married again—it was too complicated and I didn't want the responsibilities. I just wanted to be with friends and family, socialize, and go out and enjoy myself. I met one special man, Michael, in the arcade of my building. He played bridge and golf and we had a couple's social life. He lived with me for ten years and I took care of him during the illness that resulted in his death. For the last seven years, I've been dating a man, a friend of Michael's, who is three years older than I am, who I ran into by chance in a restaurant. He is kind and caring and has a wonderful family.

I believe a widow should think highly of herself as a human being and should ask herself what will give her pleasure, what she wants to do with the rest of her life. Yes, there will be the times that you are alone. Sometimes it's good to be alone. But you have to find your way. It's okay if you don't want to date and you just want to go out with your girlfriends—just don't sit around and mope. Do something: volunteer. Put a smile on your face. If you want to make friends, have confidence in yourself and show people you're a warm human being. If you like people, be willing to emotionally reach out to talk them and to help others. Me—I love people and I love life. Love yourself.

~ 5 ~

Grace N. — The Hole in My Heart

"Not long ago, someone asked me if I was happy. I can't be happy as I once was because the hole in my heart is irreparable, but I can be content; I can be involved in meaningful business and social activities, and always be there for my son."

Grace, a businesswoman, 70, was widowed in 2001. Her husband of 33 years had intermittently suffered from depression, and his death was a suicide, a suicide she does not think he intended.

I was 19 when I met George, who was 16 years older than me. We married two years later when I was a senior in college. He had been married prior to my meeting him and had two children from that marriage. George and I had one son together.

George was a veteran of the Korean War and had built a successful business. Despite his accomplishments, his self-concept was very fragile. He thought little of his own abilities and there were limits beyond which he just would not go. Many of George's army buddies had taken advantage of the GI Bill to go to college, but George couldn't do it. His self-worth had suffered a severe blow when after receiving straight A's, a grade-school teacher told him, "You're not smart enough to get straight A's." That was the last time he got all A's or good grades at all. During our marriage, I didn't realize that his episodes of depression were indicative of clinical depression; in hindsight, I believe that was a condition he inherited from his mother. Although I knew him better than anyone else, there was a part of him I didn't know. George's depression was characterized by lethargy and inertia; he was never mean or unkind. The guiding principle of his life was that a man takes care of his family. He was always there for Steven and me and for the children from his first marriage.

George's relationship with his mother had been toxic. He was always looking for answers and asking, "Why, why, why was my relationship with my mother so bad?" He told me that the only time his mother was kind and loving toward him was when he was sick—not the kind of illness that kills you but rather the chronic annoyances that diminish your quality of life. He always functioned in his business, but he couldn't at home. In one instance, George experienced a period of depression that lasted from when Steven was seven until he was nine. During those two years, I was both mother and father. I was the one who taught our son to ride a bike and drove him to soccer; I did everything with him. When George came out of his depression, he remarked that he felt like he didn't know his son. In fact, he had missed two years of his son's life. George had all these demons; he ran from one psychologist or psychiatrist to another. He tried everything: magnets on the bed, ashram, special diets, removal of metal dental fillings, whatever, to get out from under the "gray cloud." He was also self-medicating, although he hid that from me because of my abhorrence of drugs. After his death, I filled a bag with bottles of pills that I found throughout the house.

George and I had different but complementary personalities. He needed my strength and I needed the stability and encouragement he gave to me. He couldn't cope with college but he enabled me to go through graduate school and get a doctoral degree. He was so proud of his son's and his wife's accomplishments. It is simply not part of my personality to be depressed. At George's request, I stopped working when Steven was in high school as I realized that I had to be the mainstay at home and take over dual parenting roles. George's 60's were the best years of his life. He had retired and turned his business over to his oldest son. He did interesting, enjoyable things with his buddies. Then, when he was about 68, he developed problems with his foot. He was a hypochondriac and the foot problems spiraled him back into depression. There were other intermittent signs of depression. When looking at colleges for Steven, he said, "I cannot do this." It dredged up his past. So I drove thousands of miles with our son looking at colleges. This second period of depression lasted a year or two, up until his death, but I never thought he was suicidal. It was something he never wanted to discuss. He was absolutely horrified when I wanted to discuss buying cemetery plots so that we could be buried along with my parents and grandfather. He hid his inner life. I took care of the things he could not cope with.

One Saturday I was going to drive to Amish country to have a window frame repaired. Despite my practically begging him to go with me, George said he couldn't go. When I arrived home, the house was dark. I found that George had shot himself. I don't believe my husband intended to die on the day he died; I believe it was accidental. He was self-medicating and I found a bag filled with pills in the house. A knowledgeable friend went through the pills and said, "This is the one that killed him. You take that, and the mind and hand don't coordinate anymore. With a gun in his hand, his finger moved faster than his mind."

I was shocked and devastated. I couldn't believe that I would never see or touch my husband again. I was concerned about my son. I called my son's college and the college told him. I paid $600 for a cab to drive him home from his school. Steven stayed home for two to three weeks before returning to college. I went up every weekend for the rest of the term to be with him. The college provided a counselor. I saw and felt my son's grief and I suspect he was angry. I never felt any anger towards my husband. How could I be angry? For 35 years he was there for me, gave me everything in his power that he could give, and took care of his family. His death wasn't long after 9/11 and I looked at all the 9/11 grieving families—women with small children, and people who had lost family members. I had had my husband for 34 years. Relatively speaking, their loss was greater than mine. I felt he had held on for us until he was 70.

George had provided for us financially. There were assets and investments but no income. That was a problem. I needed cash flow to provide for my son and me. I sat down one night with a list of the investments and piles of forms. I thought, I don't understand this, but I've got to understand this. My son's and my future depend on my understanding this, so I stopped crying and determined to figure it out. A woman needs to be involved in her family's finances while her husband is alive. Women have to learn about money and managing money. We have to be strong and strength comes from financial well-being.

The biggest problem after George died was grief. I attended a suicide support group at a local hospital for three or four months. There were people who had been in the group for eight to ten years. I remember thinking that I wasn't going to be in a support group five, ten, fifteen years from now. I was going to get beyond this. I want to live. But being in the support group was good, and it did help. You see that other people can cope, but you also see that perhaps they aren't coping as well as they could be.

Children make coping an absolute imperative. There's a terrible sadness about children without a father. Your child's pain is as hard to bear as your own, but their well-being is your reason for going forward. After a while, I learned that I had to have a life for my son's sake—otherwise, he'd be emotionally tethered to me forever. My son was not and could not be an emotional replacement for my husband.

About a year and a half after George died, I realized I had to start building a life for myself. During that year and a half, I realized that my life had changed. Most of the people I knew were married people, and now I was a single woman so I didn't fit in anymore. I made a list of what I liked and didn't like and what I wanted more of in my life. What did I want to avoid? I wanted to avoid women-only activities, things like excessive eating and/or shopping. I focused on the positive things. I wanted more music in my life, so I bought a piano even though I didn't know how to play. Within two years, I learned to play "Moonlight Sonata." It was hard finding people to fill up night-time activities, especially weekend nights, which can be lonely. I started expanding my circle of friends. I had a friend who got me involved in English country dancing, which I loved! I learned that I didn't want to go to activities held in bars—that's a whole different scene and it wasn't for me. I went to dances in churches or in meeting halls without alcohol where you can be totally comfortable as a single woman.

After a couple years I was open to meeting men. I went to an expensive dating service and met a wonderful man who was thirteen years older. He wanted to get married but I didn't want to. I enjoyed ten wonderful years with him. He's in a retirement community now but I'm still in touch with him. Not long ago, someone asked me if I was happy. I can't be happy as I once was because the hole in my heart is irreparable, but I can be content; I can be involved in meaningful business and social activities, and always be there for my son.

Now that I'm 70 I've learned I can say no to anything I don't want to do, except paying taxes or parking tickets. I've learned that unless it's a family member, I don't do weddings. My husband loved weddings, and would actually tear up during the ceremony. I say no to weddings because you're going to sit by yourself; I find them unpleasant, even dismal. What I will sometimes do is go to the ceremony but respond that I cannot stay for the reception. You have to learn that you can say no.

When a person dies, you want the world to take notice, but it doesn't. It doesn't stop for a nano-second and there's no reason it should. Life goes on. Life is for the living; it's not for the dead. I intentionally make sure a couple of bills still arrive in his name. It hurts to see people pass away that were links to him. And, I am still struck by the fact that in the case of suicide you never get the chance to say goodbye.

I feel no guilt over whether I should have been more sensitive to nuances in my husband's behavior. If I hadn't left him alone that day, maybe things would have been different, but if someone is determined, you can't stop them. This is what many people have told me. After his death, I was struck by the number of people I knew who shared stories of suicide in their families. I know that my husband loved me and thought of me as the best wife he could have. He wrote a note and left it for me. No one will ever take my husband's place. As I've said, I was never angry at my husband for his death. He always took care of us. He was so afraid of dying—that's why I know he didn't want to kill himself that day, and that his suicide was accidental. But he was also deathly afraid of getting really old; this man was in a place where there was no peace. As part of the epitaph on my husband's tombstone, I had inscribed "He gave so much and asked for so little. A truly good man." That's what he was.

~ 6 ~

Barbara Kretchmar — Putting One Foot in Front of the Other Became My Mantra

"No one emotion can describe my anguish, my anger, grief, sadness, fear or loneliness. No one emotion because all these emotions were simultaneously riding high."

I was too young to be a widow, and Ed was too young to die. I was 46 with two young sons when Ed, 47, died of cancer in 1990. But cancer didn't care that he was only 45 when he was diagnosed in 1988 with a brain tumor that had metastasized from his lung, or that he had two young boys, then 12 and 10. Surgery successfully removed the brain tumor but the lung tumor was inoperable because of its location. Ed underwent radiation and chemotherapy and we were nervously optimistic. After several good months came several months of pain that tests and doctors were unable to diagnose. As he awaited diagnostic surgery, he suffered a minor stroke. Specialists from various departments of at the major teaching hospital performed more tests, only to discover that cancer had not only spread to his spinal column, he was also diagnosed with non-infectious marantic endocarditis, a very rare condition that most oncologists never encounter in their professional careers. It threw off tiny blood clots throughout Ed's body and was the cause of his pain that the doctors had been unable to diagnose. It would later become more virulent, triggering one major stroke after another and ultimately causing Ed to go into a coma and then die at the age of 47. A wonderful husband and a fabulous father, a ten in looks, brains and integrity, was dead.

There I was with our two sons—Jamie, 13, and Tommy, not yet 12—and no parents, no siblings, no close family. No one emotion can describe my anguish: my anger, grief, sadness, fear, loneliness. No one emotion because these emotions were all simultaneously riding high.

I was angry—damned angry. Two therapists told me I was angry at Ed for dying. Wrong, wrong, wrong! I wasn't angry at Ed, who had fought valiantly to stay alive for his sons and me; I was angry at God. I still am. I had thought that there was a just and compassionate God. My father had died when he was 51 and I was 14. He had had his first heart attack when I was just six months old, and my mother and her sister, not thinking of the effect it would have on me, kept warning me that my father could have another heart attack and die. I remember crying myself to sleep at night when I was four and five years old, afraid that my father, who was out of town on business, would be having a heart attack and dying. My biggest fear in life had been that I was going to marry a man who would die young—I had even told Ed that when we were dating. Now Ed had died at a younger age than my father and my children were fatherless at a younger age than I. My husband had been a good man, a righteous man, who had led an exemplary life. The world needed more Ed Kretchmars, not fewer. I had never met a person with more integrity than my husband—a man who was devoted to his family, his profession, his community. Odd but true: the man who behaved like a silly child when he had a common cold, never once complained or felt sorry for himself throughout his battle with cancer. Where was God? I read Kushner's *When Bad Things Happen to Good Pe*ople; to me, it was just a white paper on God that offered no rational or acceptable answers. Neither my rabbi nor religion could provide me with any answers or comfort. I lost whatever faith I had in God, and that faith has never been restored.

Twenty-eight years later, a lot of my anger at God still remains. I just am grateful that I have lived long enough to raise my children.

Like every other widow who loved her husband, I grieved for Ed. It hurt, and still does, that this wonderful father wasn't going to see his sons grow up. Just days before Ed had his first crippling stroke he asked me how many more months until Tommy's Bar Mitzvah. It hurt that he was contemplating his mortality. Never—not for one minute—did we discuss the subject of him dying, and that's because we simply maintained an optimistic attitude. But now Ed was dead. He was buried in the new suit and red tie he had bought for Jamie's Bar Mitzvah just two months earlier. The funeral parlor staff was probably more than a little surprised at the red BVDs I provided for Ed's burial outfit but that was an inside joke between Ed and me. I used to say that Ed's midlife crisis consisted of buying BVDs in every shade of every color sold: he liked to match his BVDs to whatever tie he had on that day. So we buried in him in a red tie and red BVDs ... along with a love note from me in the inside pocket of his suit jacket. Ed was buried on a cold March day. I remember going to bed that night crying, thinking of him lying in that cold, cold ground. I felt he could sense the cold and it grieved me so much. And, yes, I am crying as I write this.

I was overcome with the unfairness of life. I cried and cried for Ed, as I felt he deserved a better fate. A consummate father who took an equal role in parenting, who spent quality time with the boys, wasn't going to live to enjoy his sons growing up to become men—their graduations, their weddings, their successes. It wasn't fair to Ed or to the boys. For my sake, but especially for my sons' sake, I wanted Ed be remembered and respected for the fine person and father that he was. Although I have never considered myself a spiritual person, I tried to derive some comfort by thinking that he was proudly watching his sons' high school, college, and law school graduations and other successes from above.

Of course, I experienced loneliness and isolation (and endured the stupid remarks of some well-intentioned but emotionally insensitive comforters). I had many good friends and wonderful colleagues but I had no sisters and brothers, no close family members. Although I searched in the early 1990s, no outreach group existed for young widows. I was alone with the reality of being a young widow and of being my sons' only parent. I grieved for my sons. I had been so devastated when I lost my father at 14 that I could only imagine my children's feelings and fears. I cried in front of them so that they would know they could openly express their emotions. Although I knew how much they loved their father, they never cried in front of me—and that worried me. I elected to go to counseling, and I offered it to my sons, but they rejected it. I knew it was of the utmost importance that I keep the warmth and stability of our former life alive while showing them that life had to go on. Within three months of Ed's death, I overcame my fear of driving and got my driver's license. Instead of taking our regular beach vacations, we traveled to new places and had new adventures after summer camp was over. Episcopal Academy, the private school both boys attended from kindergarten through twelfth grade was an important factor in providing that stability. And our wonderful Helen, our daytime "babysitter," was also a stabilizing force: she was with us from the time Jamie was six months old until Tommy turned 16, and she was seated right next to us at Ed's funeral, their Bar Mitzvahs and their high school graduations. Stability? Sense of security? I could never stop worrying that something might happen to me that would leave my children parentless. I was petrified every time I had to get on a plane to travel for work. I cried for the boys because I knew the pain of being a fatherless child. I tried hard to be both mother and father, surrounding them with love while also acting as a marine drill sergeant. I pitied them, knowing it was not easy having the very loving but neurotic, crazy, sometimes screaming me as their only parent; I was tough but I was afraid to be anything else. Sure, there were some minor problems—their not doing their homework or being mouthy or arguing with each other—but they never acted out, and never drank or did drugs. They are my heroes.

I went back to work as an attorney for Scott Paper Company one week after Ed died. No company could have been more understanding or better to me during Ed's illness. Scott didn't require me to return to work so soon after Ed's death but I did it for my own sanity. I knew that life had to resume some normalcy. I knew that I had to put one foot in front of the other and keep going. I had to. There was no other way for the boys and me to survive unless I set an example. "Put one foot in front of the other" became my mantra.

There were especially hard occasions—Tommy's Bar Mitzvah was one. I was seeing two therapists to get through what should have been a very happy occasion, but one where Ed's absence was palpable. It was hard going with Tommy to pick out his Bar Mitzvah suit; that was something that Ed, as his father, should have been involved in. And there were a couple of beyond insensitive and just plain stupid remarks I had to endure. One now ex-friend was particularly irritating during my grief: as I came out of the ladies room at the hotel where Tommy's Bar Mitzvah luncheon reception was being held, she told me that I wasn't allowed to cry as that would embarrass the guests. I was fed up with her remarks and told her, in my own inimitable style, "I will do whatever the fuck I feel like doing." Jamie's graduation from Episcopal was another tough occasion. Besides seeing a therapist, I also consulted the Chaplain at Episcopal, Reverend Jim Squire, a wonderful and wise man. He told me that for some people important events like graduations are joyous occasions, whereas for others they are just something to get through. Such true words. I went with a posse to graduation night, including of course, our beloved Helen. I was concentrating so hard on getting through the graduation service itself that I never thought about which graduates might receive which awards. Then Tommy remarked, "I wonder how many awards Jamie will win." As it turned out, Jamie who could have cared less about receiving awards received six, more than any other senior at this highly competitive school. I just sat there crying, thinking to myself, "Ed, I know you're watching this from above." And I know he was there with us and very proud watching Tommy's graduation from law school and admittance to the New York Bar. As I've said, I don't consider myself religious or spiritual, but whenever I visit Ed's grave, I ask him to watch over us.

I've mentioned that I felt very alone when Ed died. I had no interest in dating, and I didn't care if I entertained or had a social life again. I remember finding a wonderful Waterford salad bowl at an antique shop—and I am obsessed with Waterford. I thought, "Why should I buy this? I'm never going to entertain again." But I did buy it. A few months after Ed died and while I was still deeply grieving for him, I also felt that urge to keep on living life, to feel socially and sexually alive. I knew Ed would have approved, and would encourage me. He would say that no one could have been a better wife all the while he was sick; he would tell me that I was young and I should keep on living and that were the situation reversed, he would try to go on with his life while still loving me. I started dating several months after Ed died and I never felt guilty. My dating was in no way disrespectful of Ed; it was a life-affirming measure for me. I was especially struck the other day when I realized that it's been more than twenty-eight years since he died and I have been a widow. Although I refused to even entertain the thought of remarrying while the boys were still at home—no man was going to tell me how to raise my children—it's been a lot of years since they have left home and I still have not remarried. I've dated a lot of interesting men, some of whom were important to me, and have had a lot of fun, but none of the relationships ended in marriage. I can't say that I really know why. Did I intentionally date the wrong men, men who looked great on paper but were not right for me? One man, with whom I was quite serious, suggested that I intentionally dated men who were not emotionally available. Perhaps deep down, subconsciously, I didn't want to remarry.

When Ed died, I recognized life had changed. I wanted to keep my very wonderful and wide circle of friends but I knew, and it became obvious, that I no longer fit into their couples' lives as I had before and that my life and my social world would have to expand. I had to make a new life that included new friends and new activities. Tennis and squash provided excellent outlets, as they were new and healthy pursuits that provided exercise, concentration, and the opportunity to extend my circle of friends and social activities. In fact, tennis and squash were indispensable. Ed and I had belonged to several clubs in Philadelphia, so I stepped up my activities in those, joining new clubs and groups to meet new people and keep myself busy. I was fortunate that I was financially able to do that and to broaden my life.

It's now almost 29 years later. I have raised two wonderful and successful sons with whom I have an excellent relation-ship. We share stories about Ed and it still gives me joy when

they or I run into someone who knew Ed and tells "Ed stories."
I am lucky to have an active life and a wide network of friends
of all ages from all phases of my life; still, I still get jealous
and misty-eyed when I see older couples walking hand-in-hand
through Rittenhouse Square. It was a future that I had envi-
sioned for Ed and me—one that was not to be.

~ 7 ~

Buntzie Churchill —
I Was and Am
Most Fortunate

"…I didn't know anything about our finances. I didn't even know where the safe deposit box was or what insurance policies there were… and most importantly, where the tuition money was hiding."

Buntzie Churchill, now in her late 70's, was 55 at the time of her husband's death in 1994. For most of her career, she was the head of the World Affairs Council of Philadelphia, a highly respected educational organization dedicated to informing and engaging people on significant national and international matters.

*P*ete was 60 when our daughter, 17, found him lying on the kitchen floor. We rushed him to the hospital. As we awaited word from the doctor, I threw my cigarettes and gold Elsa Peretti lighter in a trash can and said to my daughter, "You need a parent." I never smoked another cigarette. After waiting an hour and a half to learn from the doctor that Pete could not be resuscitated, my daughter said, "I watched my mother become a widow."

At the time of Pete's death, our marriage was pleasant and mellow, though I wondered whether, given our increasingly divergent interests, it would endure after our son and daughter were in college and instead of being a couple we would become just two people living in a big house.

After Pete's death, I was grieving, but my focus had to be on my daughter, who was a senior in high school. She had just broken up with her first boyfriend and was reeling from the loss of the two most important men in her life. She was admitted to the Ivy League college of her choice; it wasn't until her junior year that she realized she had been using her father's death as an excuse for not working up to her optimum. Then in her senior year she got straight A's in her philosophy major.

In my case, I dealt with grief by not dealing with it. Between raising my kids and fulfilling professional responsibilities, I didn't spend much time crying. My life had not stopped, and I still had things to do.

As is my nature, the first thing I did after Pete's death was to get organized. Despite my education and professional expertise, I didn't know anything about our finances. I didn't even know where the safe deposit box was or what insurance policies there were—and most importantly, where the tuition money was hiding. I had to redo all financial documents and instruments, including replacing my mother, who was becoming mentally incapacitated at 94, as the executor of my will and my children's guardian. This was an example of the way not to handle financial matters. I was the poster child for the trust company with whom I was consulting on what *not* to do. One not so minor bit of advice: get at least 24 copies of your husband's death certificate.

Grief manifests itself in many ways. At some point after Pete's death, I decided I had to change the bedroom from our bedroom to my bedroom, so I decorated it in pink. That lasted about four months! It would take approximately a year for me to get comfortable with disposing of Pete's clothes. I learned that I had to stop shopping at the local Acme because every time I would walk down an aisle, I would see things that would remind me of Pete. I learned that the car was the best place to cry as it was the most private. I remember wishing my eyeglasses had windshield wipers that would clear away the tears.

Certain memories will never fade. Pete was an expert skier and in designing his tombstone we had a likeness of him on his skis, resting on his poles, done in black cameo on the back of the tombstone. One wintry day I visited his grave, and from afar it looked as if Pete were actually standing there. It was both startling and wonderful—and then my daughter handed me a stone to place on the headstone as is the Jewish custom.

Dating was an experience. On my first date, the man and I went to the movies and he actually wouldn't share the popcorn. What a jerk! And having someone hold my hand for the first time was strange—I wasn't ready.

Then an exceptional man came to occupy a place in my life—a professor of Near Eastern Studies at Princeton University, Bernard Lewis. I had known him for about five years as a friend and he wisely waited about a year and a half before making his move. Because we had been friends, moving into a romance wasn't hard—in fact, it was delicious. That special relationship has lasted for twenty-plus years. This extraordinary man is more than 100 years old now and his memory is poor. The intellectual stimulation may be gone but the intimacy and emotional closeness is very much there. It's not so bad being told "I love you" in 15 languages.

I was and am most fortunate.

~ 8 ~

Marilyn S. — How Was I Going to Spend the Rest of My Life?

"I was at a business dinner in New York City when I got the phone call that Warren had died… I was so relieved. It was over. He had been so sick, but now he was at peace. A huge burden had been lifted, and I was so happy for him."

Marilyn, a career marketing executive and mother of three, now in her early 60's, was 49 when her husband died in 2003 after being diagnosed with cancer four years earlier.

*W*arren, the father of my children, actually died long before he died; he was breathing but the husband and father we knew and loved was gone. He was a heavy smoker and drinker who was diagnosed with Stage 4 esophageal cancer at 44. We had been married for 21 years and had three children: a son, 20, a daughter, 18, both in college, and another daughter, 16, who was in high school. At first we were very optimistic because he was young and otherwise generally healthy and the cancer was focused in the throat and not in a major organ. But about six months later there was a recurrence of the tumor in or around the voice box. He had major surgery, which meant a very long recovery, an artificial speech aid, and intensive speech training.

After the surgery, Warren's whole life changed, and he lost his ability to do many of the things he loved most—play golf, do his job, and be a buddy to all his good friends and neighbors. He aged rapidly and seemed to become an old man. He was angry and in denial until almost the day he died. My role as wife diminished and my role as caretaker began. At first he seemed to have improved. He was weak and although eating was difficult for him, we could go out to restaurants and to family parties. Eventually he needed a stomach tube to sustain nutrition: eating, drinking and swallowing were very difficult. He was often too depressed to eat or share meals with us. During this time, while in radiation treatments, Warren began smoking again. This was so dangerous and could reverse all the effects of the treatments. The children and I were shocked and concerned. After I caught him smoking, we separated for six months. After counseling, he started taking better care of himself.

Two and a half years after the initial diagnosis, the doctors found another tumor near the carotid artery that was inoperable and untreatable. Warren's diagnosis was now terminal. Our original optimism turned to facing the reality that his time was limited. Warren's condition became a matter of pain management, and he spent nine months in hospice care.

There were days that I thought he wasn't going to make it. He was so very sick—it was hard to breathe, hard to move. The hospice nurse and the aides didn't have much hope as time was very short. We didn't think he would make it until Christmas but he did. For over a year, we knew he was going to die but we didn't know when. I would wake up and ask myself, "Is this the day?" Then days, weeks and months would go by and I would ask, "Is he ever going to die. Is this the way we're going to live? Will it ever end?"

As a family, we understood it would be good for Warren to let go. The kids would come home on weekends and go upstairs to see him individually to tell him that it was okay to let go. I was also trying to tell him that it was okay to let go, but he was withdrawing. He was so depressed and would often stay in the bedroom and refuse to talk to us. I was worried that he might die before he let the kids know how much he loved them, how much they meant to him, so we could have some closure. I told him, "We're all dying every day. You really have to think what message you want to leave your children." But he was convinced death was the end of everything. He really believed he had no spirit; he thought that when he died, wherever he was buried, that was the end of him.

In those four years of his illness, death was occurring all the time. I come from an Italian Catholic family where we get our strength from our faith in God. I was a churchgoer and during those four years, I prayed every day. I went to church on Sunday and as often as I could. The oldest of six kids, I was always the strong one, the survivor. I tried to be as realistic and pragmatic as I could. I really believed that although Warren's illness might not end well, we would manage our way through it. My faith, my family and my friends helped me to take one day at a time and keep going. I felt it was important that I be the strong one for my husband and my children, and that I set a good example.

Because of Warren's tremendous pain and high levels of medication, I agreed with the hospice staff to move him to a nursing facility. At this stage, I authorized the medical staff to use its best judgment to provide as much comfort as possible and to give Warren whatever medication would be of help during his last days. He remained in the nursing home for three weeks with no food or water, on high levels of pain medication. Eventually he became very anxious and it was too challenging for the staff to care for him. He was moved to the local hospital for a change of medication that could only be administered there. The change in medication was prescribed to reduce the anxiety, but we realized that with every transition, death could come at any time.

Two days later, I was at a business dinner in New York City when I got the phone call from my sister-in-law that Warren had died. His brother had been with him when he passed peacefully while they were watching baseball, one of his favorite sports. I was so relieved. It was over. He had been so sick, but now he was at peace. A huge burden had been lifted, and I was so happy for him.

The next morning, I returned home on the train with my son who lived in the City, and my daughters flew home from Boston. We were all mentally prepared for Warren's passing. We had talked about it, thought about it and waited for it. Other people might not understand but we understood why he had to go. My youngest daughter remarked, "I understand it but I can't stop crying." We talked about the funeral. We decided we would all carry water bottles in honor of their Dad. Warren had carried one with him all the time because the radiation caused his throat to be so very dry. If we got emotional or choked up, we could take a sip. The biggest source of sadness during the funeral preparation was caused by my mother-in-law. It was heartbreaking. At first she said she would not make the trip for the funeral. Her sisters talked to her and convinced her to come to share her sadness with our children, her grandchildren and to honor her son's life. Our kids were great—they were so strong. I didn't feel sorry for myself at the time. And the death and burial procedure provided a sense of closure for everyone who loved Warren. It was a beautiful spring day when we buried and honored my husband. My children and I will never forget that day.

When I became a widow, I knew life had to go on. I do think Warren's death would have been much harder for me to recover from if he had suddenly died unexpectedly rather than dying after a prolonged illness. I did feel cheated as to the future we could have had, but I knew that life goes forward. During Warren's illness and after his death, there was only so much I could share with my family. My support was a couple of really close girlfriends, my sister-in-law and my kids. My kids were my rock. I had to be strong; I had to find sources of strength, people who would listen, people who would work through his death with me. I went and found out how other people had dealt with death of a spouse. I was worried that I would forget Warren—that was a big concern of mine. Because of my children and their memories, the funny stories and our holiday rituals, when we missed him most, I soon knew I didn't have to worry about Warren being forgotten.

For a few months after the funeral, the hardest thing was coming home to an empty house. When I married, I went straight from my parents' home to the one I shared with my husband, so I had never come home to an empty house. Then I had to contemplate what I was going to do with the rest of my life. I had spent my whole life doing what I had to: raising my children, taking care of my home, loving my husband and family. I realized my life was no longer about my kids, as they were grown and able to take care of themselves. Yes, I had my job but I didn't know what I wanted to do in my personal life. I liked to go to the movies and out to dinner but I didn't have any hobbies. My daughter encouraged me to redecorate the house, to make the rooms my own. I did that and it was sort of fun. To thank the kids and to let them know how proud I was of them, I decided to treat them and used some of the insurance money to take them to Europe. It was a trip their Dad had very much wanted to take, but he was too ill in those last years. We went during Thanksgiving because it was such an emotional holiday, one that my husband was so much a part of. It was the right thing to do for all of us and we talked about Warren a lot during the trip. To hear the kids telling all those funny and touching stories about their Dad, keeping his memory alive, has always been a big source of comfort to me. I can feel Warren's impact on their lives and his legacy.

But the big question still remained: how was I going to spend the rest of my life? One of my professional colleagues had relocated to Italy and invited me to visit. I went and had a wonderful time. On the nine-hour flight home, I realized I didn't have to do anything I didn't want to. I realized how short life can be and how Warren had regretted not getting to do those special things he wanted to do with his life. He had advised the children and me to learn from his experience. I decided to quit my job, which I didn't really like anymore, and to do something I had wanted to do—start a consulting business. I felt a renewed sense of self because I realized that I could choose to do what I wanted. I also realized that I could be by myself and live a single life.

I never felt that my married friends dropped me after Warren had died. The couples' part of our social life had already lessened while Warren was alive because it was difficult for him to go out and socialize. After he died, I would do things with my girlfriends and would go to parties with my married friends. But even though I'm not a shy person, I felt strange being by myself. I would force myself to go but I felt incomplete.

People were asking me if I had thought about dating. At 50, I felt young and healthy. I knew I could not keep living my life as if I didn't know what I was going to do. About a year and a half after Warren's death, I saw a church bulletin about a social for widowed people and singles and decided to attend. I met someone whom I dated for six months. I was glad for companionship. I didn't feel guilty with regard to Warren because if the situation had been reversed, I would have expected him to go on living and to move forward. But I did feel uncomfortable about the kids, as they were so devoted to Warren. I didn't tell them for a long time. It turned out that they didn't like the man I was dating and I realized that they were right. After breaking up with him, I went to another church social that was absolutely hideous. I then heard about Match.com from a friend and gave it a try. About two years after Warren died, I met the man I've now been dating for ten years. He's different from Warren. He's a recovered alcoholic and he doesn't smoke. I couldn't be with someone now who can't control his alcohol or smoking. The girls liked him immediately, though my son was uncertain at first. My son has always been very protective of me. Because he's the oldest, he witnessed more of the hurt, pain and loss over the years. He's a man and he was his father's best friend, so he knew his father better than the rest of us. Today we all get along fabulously. This other man is not their father, but he is their friend. And I didn't have to worry: Warren's memory remains in our hearts and in our lives always.

I would encourage grieving widows to ask for help and advice and to seek out those friends and confidantes who have lived through your experience. Know that you are not alone, but one of a very large and special group of strong, thriving women. With support, you can lift yourself up and pay it forward.

~ 9 ~

Sister Marcy — A Guiding Light

"There's a roadmap for everybody's life... Within each of us, there is a shining star, a guiding light, and if we just keep our focus and push towards that, we will find that we are more than we think we are."

In 1986 when Sister Marcy was 30, her husband, Walter, was murdered while being robbed on a Brooklyn street. He died instantly, leaving Sister Marcy with two young sons to raise.

I married my husband in 1972 when I was 16 and he was 20. My older brother had met Walter while they were in the Job Corps in Indiana and brought him to my family's home in Philadelphia during a vacation. We were soon married and moved to Brooklyn, where Walter was from originally. He worked as an electrician for the City of New York and after I graduated from a high school in Brooklyn, I worked for an insurance company.

Housing was more affordable in Philadelphia than in New York, and we thought we could both easily get good jobs there, so on October 24, 1986, I went to Philadelphia with our two sons, who were nine and ten, to look for houses. While I was there, I got the phone call that the police had found Walter murdered on a sidewalk in Brooklyn while he was being held up. It was horrific—I could never have imagined such a thing. Despite some people's skepticism about our marriage, we were determined and climbed all the mountains to make the marriage work. I always thought we would grow old together, enjoy our grandkids, and live the American Dream. His death was like a slap in the face.

After Walter's death, I went back to New York with my parents for three days to identify Walter's body at the morgue and to make funeral arrangements. When we got to New York, I found that whoever had killed Walter had also broken into our apartment, ransacked it and stole all our valuables, including our wedding pictures and our memories. The police never found the criminals who committed the murder and the burglary and this still gnaws at me today. Except for going to New York for Walter's funeral, I never took the boys back there.

There was no reason for me to remain in New York. I returned to Philadelphia and the boys and I moved in with my grandmother. The grieving process didn't go well for either the boys or me. We each grieved in our separate ways. I think I was more angry than grieving—I just shut down, and I was upset with everybody over everything. I felt that someone had violated us. I didn't want to hear anything from anybody as there was nothing they could do to change what had happened, what had been taken away from us. I was going to have to start my life all over again and I wasn't happy about that.

The boys didn't handle it well at all. At first, I don't think they understood that their father wasn't coming back. Then they blamed me for his death. My younger son, would say, "If it wasn't for you, this wouldn't have happened." I think he felt that if all four of us had been in Brooklyn that day, Walter would not have been killed. About a week after Walter's burial, the boys started changing. They each had their own grief to deal with and I think they also felt alone in their grief. I should have gotten my sons and me some help but I didn't know that help was out there or how to seek it out. I also didn't want people involved in my business. My older son, felt like, "I'm going to be the man and I'm going to do what I want to do." He started doing crazy things like breaking into people's cars. He got arrested a couple of times, and was in and out of juvenile detention facilities. This went on for several years. My younger son became a loner, staying in his room and playing games. He didn't want to engage in conversation. Both boys were not doing well in school and the younger one dropped out. When he was 17, he was arrested by the police for being in a car that had a whole cache of guns and he went to prison for six years. No one ever offered us any psychological or social services, which could have avoided some or all of this from happening. Fortunately, my boys didn't get into drugs, but unfortunately, I did. Today, both sons have turned their lives around and are doing well. Both are happily married, one with four children, own their own homes and have wonderful jobs. The younger one has been a chef at a local university for more than eleven years, while the older is a truck driver for a meat company. I think this turnaround was because eventually I became involved in the church. They started going to church with me and when I would visit them, I would talk with them about forgetting and forgiving.

I wasn't in a good place after Walter died. Not only was I very angry, I also felt that I was alone with nothing to live for. About six months or so after Walter's death, I started free basing cocaine. The boys didn't know about my drug use because I shielded them from it. I think my grandmother, a churchgoing woman, suspected, because she would say to me, "Mamma praying for you." That would make me mad; I didn't want anybody praying for me because the cocaine was making me feel good. It gave me a high that made me feel good about everything and lasted one, two or three hours. This went on for about four years, from about 1987 through 1991. My social world consisted of hanging out in the drug culture with other drug users. That culture wasn't about building relationships; it was about being with other users who could tell you where to get drugs, the best drugs. Somewhat ironically, at the same time that I was into free-basing cocaine, I attended and graduated from a vocational school for nurses' aides.

I knew I was in a bad place and I knew I could end up dead from that whole lifestyle. Around 1991, I got tired of where my life was going. I had been brought up in the church but had gotten away from it. One Sunday, by sheer happenstance, I joined my not particularly religious mother and a cousin for services at a non-denominational church, Crusaders for Christ International Ministry. It was the turning point in my life. I stopped using drugs because of a woman preacher, Apostle Thelma Malone, who saved my life. She had been a public school teacher until God told her to quit her job and go into the ministry full-time. She was responsible for 29 churches. Thelma Malone spoke to me. I think she took a special interest in me because she believed that God had a call on my life, that I had been called by God to do certain things. I listened to her when she told me, "Why don't you follow me, follow Christ.

Your life will never be the same. Follow me until you see me doing something wrong, and then walk away." She told me she wanted to see me in church on Sundays, Tuesdays, Thursdays and Fridays. She enrolled me in the Ministry's Saturday Bible Institute and its Sunday School. I also attended the Sunday 6:00 P.M. services, so I almost lived at the church. She made me read and discuss with her each day ten chapters of the Bible, Old and New Testaments. She taught me how to fulfill the will of God and to fill the spiritual part of my life, which was empty. She did missionary work. While I studied with her, she had me almost immediately visiting churches with her and she taught me how to open up churches. I was also preaching, setting up Bible studies at different churches, doing revivals, and going out on the street feeding and helping homeless people—which I still do today. I traveled to 14 different countries with Apostle Thelma and the Ministry. Until she died in 2007, Thelma Malone was, and still remains, a very strong presence in my life.

It took me 30 years to go through the process of grieving, a process that first consisted of using drugs and then religion and the church. The church was the means by which I established a new life and was the best thing that could have happened to me. I'm in a good place now. When my sons were young, I didn't want get involved in another relationship; I didn't want the emotional sadness of burying someone again. I didn't want the uncertainty of new men coming in and out of my sons' lives. I had promised my children that I would hang in there together with them, and that it would just be us. I told them I wouldn't change my last name until they were grown. But they're grown now, at 40 and 41, and I'm engaged to be married. My sons and I are thrilled. I'm engaged to a man I grew up with, whom I got to know through the church. He asked me to marry him in Bible Study one Tuesday night; we're going be married in the summer of 2017. It took quite a long time, 30 years, but I am now very happy and very satisfied with my life.

I believe God has a call for everybody. There's a roadmap for everybody's life. We will all have troubles but we're not to dwell on the negative but to push forward. Within each of us, there is a shining star, a guiding light and if we just keep our focus and push towards that, we will find that we are more than we think we are.

~ 10 ~

Shannon McAuliffe — Do You!

"But I decided that whatever I felt I needed to do, I would do. It didn't matter what anybody else thought. My motto was "Do you!" I believe it's okay to be a little self-centered."

In 2008 when Shannon McAuliffe was 40, her husband of three years, Richard Egbert, died after collapsing on a boat in the middle of a lake.

*I*n 2005, I was 37 and a public defender in Boston; Richie was 56 and a high-profile criminal lawyer who defended infamous mobsters and politicians—and judges. One day, my supervisor insisted that, for learning purposes, we attend one of Richie's trials so we could learn from the very best. We walked into a crowded courtroom and I heard this rich, booming and authoritative voice—the deepest voice I had ever heard. I looked all around, and 5'9" me was shocked to discover that the voice was coming from a short 5'5" guy—Richie. I met him for the first time after court, and I basically tripped all over myself and my words because I was so impressed with his talent. A few months later, my friend, who was his legal associate, told me that Richie was getting a divorce and I enthusiastically asked her to set me up with him. She balked, and then informed me that I was assuming a lot in expecting that Richie Egbert would want to go out with me. A month later *he* asked *her* to set us up! We double-dated. After dinner, Richie took me to a gay club that his friend owned for "foam night"—where foam suds envelop the room and you can't see the person you're dancing with. Afterwards, I spent the night ... and the next night ... at Richie's. In my mind, this was going to be a great affair with an older man. I never thought it was going to be a serious relationship until a couple of months later when he told me he was interested in a long-term future with me. We dated for about a year and a half, got engaged, and then married. We had been together for about five years when Richie died at 61.

Richie had three children from his former marriages: two married daughters, one ten years and the other five years younger than me, and a younger son. One day in the summer of 2008, while Richie's family was staying at my family's lake house in upstate New York, Richie, his son, daughters, sons-in-law, grandchildren, and I all went waterskiing on the lake.

Everyone but me had finished waterskiing and returned to the boat; I was still out in the middle of the lake about to water-ski. I saw Richie get into the boat, zip his jacket, sit down, and lean back. He almost looked as if he were playing with the grandkids, pretending to snore. But then when the boat moved, Richie fell over. The family stopped the boat, and I heard one son-in-law say, "We're going in." They returned to the dock, leaving me still in the water, at least the length of the water ski line away. I was upset but I knew the lake, so I swam to the nearest shore-line. A kayaker rowed me to a motorboat, which took me to my family's dock, where I saw Richie. As we approached, I heard sirens and saw paramedics working on an unresponsive Richie. The second I saw him on the dock, not moving, I just knew that my life would be changed forever. The rule in my head: when someone suffers a heart attack, if he can talk, then he lives, but if he can't talk, he dies. He was unconscious, and I was beside myself. We were far away from a hospital and I wanted Richie at the hospital as fast as possible. The ambulance ride to the hospital was painfully slow: the paramedics were trying to resuscitate him, and were simultaneously communi-cating with doctors at the hospital. Richie's kids were following in a separate car.

At one point, the ambulance pulled to the side of the road and a paramedic told me, "You have to call it." "Call what?" I asked. "You have to call his time of death so get the kids in here." I asked if they were sure it was necessary at this point, but then they stopped working on him. I guess the doctor at the hospital must have made the decision to call it and had told them to stop their efforts. I never got the chance to speak with Richie one last time after he collapsed and lost consciousness on the boat.

I knew my life was now going to be a deep void. I was numb and in shock but I was also very controlled and operated on automatic pilot because there were things that I had to take care of right away. Immediately after we got back to the lake house, the phone calls started, requesting us to donate Richie's body parts. Too much time had elapsed to donate his organs but his cornea, skin and muscles were harvestable. After securing his children's agreement for the donations, I then had to answer 30 minutes of bizarre questions from the requesting organizations, including, "Do you think he has had sex for a fee?" I had to attend to matters like the autopsy—his death was due to an almost completely clogged artery—and the funeral, which was scheduled for the following Monday in a Jewish synagogue, although no one in Richie's family was a practicing Jew. I also had to write and deliver a eulogy that would measure up to his greatness and everyone's love for him. Reporters in Boston learned of Richie's death and started calling. One wanted a statement about Richie, his legal career, and what his clients were now going to do. I said, "This is what you've got to get right: He was a phenomenal lawyer, but as good a lawyer as he was, he was a hundred times better father, husband, brother and friend." They printed that.

When I woke up the morning after Richie died, I wasn't sure how I was going to even live through the next three minutes. I opened my eyes and saw my mother looking at me with more pain in her eyes than I had ever seen. I could not bear to watch her watch me. She wanted to drive me back to Boston but I refused—I couldn't navigate my own pain, much less hers. Somehow I drove back the four and a half hours to Boston by myself and arrived there safely despite vacillating between crying hysterically and talking calmly on the phone to others who loved him.

I was very lucky to have amazing support—the world was supportive. Our apartment building in Boston was undergoing a massive renovation, which rendered half of our apartment unlivable. Luckily, I had thought to call our building management before driving back to Boston and tell them what had happened to Richie. The management was incredible. It pulled workmen from all over the building to work on our apartment and had it completed within five and a half hours. A friend, Eve, took a flight from Baltimore to meet me at the apartment and stay with me. Eve just lived my life for me—dressed me, fed me, told me when to go to bed and when to sign things. Everybody did everything for me. Richie's kids were amazing and we were there for each other. Everywhere I went, people knew Richie and shared in my grief but they didn't invade my privacy. Of course, there are always some people who have never experienced grief or don't know what to say. I will never forget the lawyer who told me that he couldn't believe that I had held Richie's funeral on a Monday, which had made it so inconvenient for him to attend. You almost can't even get mad when people are such idiots because you just don't have the energy for anything other than your grief.

I returned to work a week later—work was an important part of my grieving process. I needed to be at work. I couldn't just stay at home because that was too depressing. At home, I excelled at staring at walls, at doing nothing. This lasted a while.

For several months after Richie died I was just destroyed: I believed that there was no afterlife for Richie when he died. I could not fathom that someone so big in life, so bright, could be here one minute and then gone the next. It was too hopeless to believe that one minute you have life and then you don't, that you become nothing. I wanted to research where Richie and his energy had gone. I kept looking for things to tell me that he wasn't gone. I studied death from scientific articles to books to movies on the afterlife. About three months after Richie died while I was still struggling with his "goneness" and the matter of afterlife, I accepted an invitation from a friend in California to go to a spa with her for a few days. While waiting for a massage, the silver-haired Birkenstock-wearing masseuse asked, "Is there something going on with you? I know you're here for a massage but I'm a medium and I'm getting these very strong vibes. Have you lost someone recently?" When I said yes, she asked if his name started with an "R." I agreed to let the masseuse tap into this. Then it seemed as if she started having a conversation with someone. It was like she was telling Richie what I was saying and then telling me what he was replying.

She said things no one knew or could have known about our lives, especially since Richie and I had different last names and I was clear across the country. She said we would begin and I thought, "Please, please, please say something that reso-nates—say something that means something." There is no way that she could have known that Richie had a special orange pen that everyone wanted after he died, yet the first thing she said to me was, "He is holding out a pen to me." This was the single most important moment of my life because I knew he wasn't gone: he might not have been here but he was some-where and that was good enough for me. I had two questions I wanted her to ask Richie. I wanted to know if he thought I had been a good enough wife. She told me what he communicated to her: the only time he had ever lost confidence in himself and felt that he wasn't a man was when he was going through his divorce. Then he met me, and I made him believe in himself again; I made him feel like a man again; I saved him. I asked her if Richie missed me. She said that he knew I missed him and he was sorry; he said he did miss me but it wasn't the same for him. He knew that he would see me again; for him, time didn't exist, so it would be a very short period for him before he saw me again but it would be a very long period for me. This encounter with the masseuse was a turning point for me. I now felt that there was an afterlife, and that Richie was somewhere. Now I wasn't totally hopeless. I don't know what would have happened to me without that experience.

After Richie died, I went to a therapist I had seen before. I only went once, and it was awful. I didn't need someone to tell me how much Richie loved me; I needed someone to tell me what was going on with me physically, mentally, emo-tionally. I wanted someone to talk with about these issues and work through them with me. I wanted a psychiatrist, a person with a medical degree. A friend who had lost a child gave me the name of one, an Israeli woman. I saw her once a week for several months, and then tapered off to once every other week, then once a month. We worked on my guilt coupled with my fears. Guilt is the emotion I excel at. Although I'm Protestant, I did have years of Catholic schooling, and guilt was the easiest bucket to put my emotions in—that was easier for me than wrestling with how to mourn someone who doesn't exist anymore. When I started seeing her, I felt a crushing guilt about everything: we were too far away from a hospital when Richie collapsed, I wasn't a good enough wife, I didn't make him as happy as I could have, I wasn't selfless enough. I felt guilt about arguments we had had. All this guilt didn't make sense. I also felt that I was the one in charge of my pain, but I think when we're grieving, we want someone to ride the pain with us, to acknowledge that this sucks, that it's horrible. I believe my therapy sessions were very helpful because I could express all the deep dark thoughts I was feeling without someone being judgmental or trying to make me feel better. I felt that my shrink guided me through my grief but without telling me that it was going to be okay. I didn't want to hear that bromide. She told me that there was no blunting the pain: I was grieving, I was supposed to feel like this. I just had to feel the pain and go through it. She also said I wasn't depressed and refused to give me antidepressants. She said I was appropriately heartbroken and what I was feeling was normal; according to her, the grieving process was supposed to suck. After two years, she broke up with me. She told me she thought I had worked through my guilt and fears and had gone through the process of grieving. Therapy is interesting. You do all this work at the beginning and then one day you feel grounded. You feel you can now be alone with yourself. You're not thinking about all the pain all the time.

In addition to my grieving issues, I was subject to panic attacks for several months. I wasn't afraid of dying; when I had a panic attack, I felt like I was going to die at any time and I was afraid of feeling so horrible. I didn't know how I was going to get through the next minute, the next second. I told my psychiatrist about the attacks and she had me select the anti-anxiety medication that I thought worked best for me. Morning was the worst time for these attacks so I would wake up and take an Ativan and I would feel better. I never needed nor took Ativan to go to court. But I kept the pills with me and would take half a pill if I felt a panic attack coming on. I never took more than two pills a day. Then the panic attacks subsided.

After Richie's death, I supplemented my reading about an afterlife with reading books about death and grieving—that wasn't particularly helpful. The books about the various stages of grief were mostly useless, but the passage below from Joan Didion's *A Year of Magical Thinking*[1] still resonates with me:

"Grief turns out to be a place none of us know until we reach it…. We might expect if the death is sudden to feel shock. We do not expect the shock to be obliterative, dislocating to both body and mind…. Nor can we know ahead of the fact (and here lies the heart of the difference between grief as we imagine it and grief as it is) the unending absence that follows, the void, the very opposite of meaning, the relentless succession of moments during which we will confront the experience of meaninglessness itself" (pp. 188-189).[1]

As I said, the books I read weren't especially helpful to me, a young widow — I didn't think they were real enough or modern enough to resonate with other young widows or capture what we were feeling and experiencing. I think I could have benefitted from a modern girls' version of grief. Thoughts of death and grieving don't just disappear. Because I wanted to help others on their path to healing, a couple of years after Richie died, I wrote a ten-page paper about death and grieving and shared it with friends who were young widows or who had lost a child. It was a liberating experience for me and it made me feel good that those who have read it found it helpful. Writing those ten pages was hard for me but it also helped me because I believe that Richie's death, my grieving, and writing the paper helped me learn about myself.

---

[1] Joan Didion, *The Year of Magical Thinking* (Alfred A. Knopf, a Division of Random House, New York, 2006).

I usually know how to pull myself up by my bootstraps but for a long time I just couldn't make myself feel better. But I decided that whatever I needed to do, I would do. It didn't matter what anybody else thought. My motto was, "Do you!" I believe it's okay to be a little self-centered. To the people who were shocked that I went out to dinner two nights after Richie died, I said that going out to dinner was what I felt like doing. There were also nights I went out to dinner and literally cried in my soup. If I was supposed to go out to dinner and then didn't feel like it, I cancelled. I had to try to make myself feel better. About six months after Richie died, I started dating because I needed to do things that would make me feel better, even if only for the moment. Dating was a distraction. I dated a lot of too young or otherwise inappropriate men—men whom I would otherwise never have wanted to spend an evening with except that I needed to do something. Sometimes I felt good about the guy, sometimes not. It didn't matter. My energy was there. It made me feel. I needed to be in the world again. It helped me get through that horrible period. And you learn a little something from every person. I firmly believe that the grieving are entitled to forget that we are grieving, even for one night. There was also something about my body chemistry that had changed, had adapted, to get me what I psychologically wanted and needed. I became a sexier and more attractive version of myself. I had the kind of male attention that I had never had before. Two years after Richie died, I met a man I really cared for. At first I felt guilty for being happy but the relationship helped me, even though it didn't work out at the end. The relationship felt good—I felt good, I was hopeful, and I started believing in myself again. I've been in several meaningful relationships since then and am in one now.

Although I knew when I saw the paramedics working on an unconscious Richie back at the dock that my life was going to change, I didn't appreciate how much it would change. Prior to Richie's death, my circle of friends consisted mostly of my girlfriends, who were pretty much my contemporaries, and of

Richie's friends, who were an older, more mature crowd. After his death, I became very friendly with a 30-year-old woman, who was ten years younger than I. She was exactly what I needed. My old world as I had lived it was gone and she introduced me to her world, a world new to me, made up of young, smart, charming people who cared about their bodies, their clothes, and vacations. She dressed me up, took me out and put me in a new, different space. I learned I was still desirable and valuable. She reinvented me and I will always be grateful to her. I still had my great longstanding friends but the freshness and newness of a different, younger crowd was perfect; it was exactly what I needed to fill an itty bitty portion of the void.

Very importantly, with my psychiatrist's encouragement, I created a new life for myself in another way. Before Richie died, I was always on a quest for knowledge, and was interested in my personal growth and desired to better myself. When he died, the drive I once had was extinguished and I didn't know if I was going to get it back. A friend kept telling me that I was still me, that I would get back to being me. I seriously questioned if that were true. What changed my attitude? I had told my psychiatrist that at one time I wanted to change careers and attend Harvard's Kennedy School, but I doubted I could get in. My psychiatrist thought that was a great idea and encouraged me to go for it. Although it took me two or three years to actually apply, I did apply in 2012. When I made the decision to apply, I realized that this was something I wanted very badly. I studied really hard and worked my butt off to get in. That's when I knew I had turned the corner. Building a new career gave me a totally new lease on life. Fellow students at the Kennedy School didn't know who my husband had been and they didn't care that I was a lawyer. I worked hard and excelled. When Richie died, I didn't know how I could live my life without seeing myself reflected in his eyes. When he looked at me, I would feel like the most special, beautiful, smart and loved person. He could take my faults and make them into compliments. Being seen through Richie's eyes gave me confidence.

When I no longer had him to look at me that way, I wondered who I was. But then I got into this new career where I excelled, and I loved it. I was a superstar on my own; I didn't need Richie for me to be or feel like a superstar. That was a huge part of my transformation. Now I have a totally different life as Director of Roca—an innovative, one-stop get-your-life-together nonprofit program that interrupts the cycle of poverty and incarceration by intervening in high-risk young men's lives. It's an exciting life, one I would have always dreamed of, but I'm not sure that I would have realized it if Richie were still alive.

I do have some thoughts I would like to share with grieving widows. Everything you feel is valid. The pain is so crushing, so excruciating, and you can't fix it. You have to feel what you feel when you feel it. And you should feel what you want. When you don't know what you want, consider seeking professional help. There's no timeline, no stages. It takes as long as it takes and it takes a long time. You have to be kind to yourself. You are allowed to be selfish: you can do whatever you want, you don't have to do things that other people think you should.

~ 11 ~

Carol Iamurri —
I Wasn't Afraid
of Raising a Child Alone

"Interestingly, in spite of Donny's death at 21, I never thought of my own mortality or its consequences for my daughter."

Carol Iamurri was 21 and four months pregnant when her soldier husband was killed in an Army barracks in 1969 while waiting to be deployed to Vietnam.

I was raised in a strict Catholic household and attended private Catholic schools until I graduated when I was 17. I wanted to attend an out-of-town four-year college, but my mother insisted that I attend a community college where I would come home every day after school. Instead, I went to work.

In 1965, when I was 18, a friend introduced me to Donny, who was six months older than me. He was funny, intelligent, nurturing and came from a good family. We clicked. When we met, he worked with his father as a welder in the Philadelphia Navy Yard. He knew that he would soon be drafted to go to Vietnam. Donny proposed to me in 1967, right after he received his draft notice, and we got engaged. That summer, he reported for duty at Ft. Dix in New Jersey before being transferred to Ft. Carlson in Colorado. Because I wanted to get married before Donny went to Vietnam, we were married on November 23, 1968. The following morning, we started our drive to Ft. Carson. We had so much fun, with him showing me the country. I had never been further than the Jersey shore. We had our Thanksgiving dinner at some generic diner, but it was the best Thanksgiving meal I ever had. Actually, we were then in the Midwest, and our waitress told me that I had a very "strange" accent. What did I know? Everyone in Philly spoke like me! We lived in a renovated Victorian house in Colorado Springs. Each of its four apartments housed a military couple and the landlord lived in the basement. Each couple paid $3.00 a month for the privilege of using the common telephone to make local calls. We were very happy. Because I didn't want to get pregnant right after we were married, I went to a doctor in January to learn about and begin a birth control regimen. After examining me, I was stunned when the doctor told me that I was six weeks pregnant. I was a virgin when I was married—that didn't stop family members from counting backwards!

In March, the Army transferred Donny to the Mojave Desert for a 38 day training period so he would be well-prepared to use English tanks when he was sent to Vietnam. The training period would be followed by two weeks of leave before he would be deployed. On the second or third day in Colorado Springs, when I happened to close my eyes for a moment, I saw a vision of a casket. Donny wasn't scheduled to go to Vietnam for another two months. I tried to erase this horrible vision from my mind. I went to church, I prayed for our marriage, for Donny's safety, and then I successfully put it out of my mind. Two weeks later at 3:00 A.M., our landlord knocked on my door to tell me there was a phone call for me. I thought, "That Donny, he's such a goofball, he's waking me up at 3:00 A.M. to tell me he loves me." Instead, I found myself talking to a military officer; he put an Army chaplain on the phone who told me that Donny had been involved in an accident. A soldier in Donny's barracks was fooling around with a gun, harassing another solder. Donny never liked bullies, so he had intervened to protect the frightened, bullied soldier, and the bully's gun discharged, and Donny got shot. I was told, "He's at death's door." Donny would be medevac'd to Letterman Army Hospital in San Francisco for treatment and travel arrangements were being made to fly me to San Francisco to be with Donny. I didn't want to call and frighten either Donny's or my parents at 3:00 A.M. with this news, so I sat there by myself, just 21, and four months pregnant, frozen in my chair, for four hours until 7:00 A.M. when I called his parents. I told them that Donny had been involved in an accident and the Army wanted us to go to San Francisco to be with him; I didn't tell them that he had been shot. I then called my parents and my father said we would all meet in San Francisco.

In San Francisco, we were told that Donny had been shot in the aorta—in those days, a death sentence. Amazingly, he lived for nine days. During those nine days, he was medicated and received continuous blood transfusions. He would fade in and out of consciousness. When conscious, he would say, "As soon as I'm out of here, babe, we'll have a big party," and I would agree with him. He was optimistic; he didn't know he didn't have a chance. Even though I had been told he was at death's door, every time he opened his eyes, I thought, "He's lucid, he's so strong, there's a chance." I was too dumb to know he wasn't going to survive. Nine days later, I received a 5:00 A.M. phone call to come to the hospital: the end was near. Then Donny was dead.

Since he was a healthy 21-year-old, I wanted to donate his organs but I deferred to his parents. Although his father was the best of men, he objected because he wanted his son's body to remain intact. I asked, "Dad, just one favor. Can we donate his corneas? It won't deform his eyes or the way he looks, but it will help some wounded soldier to see." My father-in-law agreed. Donny had a huge funeral back in New Jersey. I had never been to a funeral before. I couldn't handle seeing Donny in an open casket; I didn't want to remember him that way. I explained to my in-laws that I didn't want to hurt them, that it was just my intention to take care of myself, and I didn't think I could handle seeing Donny in the customary open casket. I asked them whether we couldn't have a closed casket with pictures of him next to the casket while I was there. My in-laws agreed and anyone who wanted to see Donny in an open casket could do so during designated times when I wasn't present.

I had five months of my pregnancy to get through until I was due to deliver our baby. How did I get through it? I know I was numb. Other than that, I don't remember too much. I couldn't take sedatives because I was pregnant. My best medicine was my in-laws. I spent a lot of time with Donny's family because they were so loving and I felt safe with them. Religion didn't help me much in the grieving process. Despite my strict Catholic upbringing, I didn't try to find solace in the Catholic Church—I wasn't comfortable there. I didn't go to church but I prayed to God to get through this, to have a healthy baby, to make my baby happy. They were Catholic prayers but I added my own prayers to God as well. I wanted to believe in my own spirituality. I also secretly prayed for a girl. I was afraid that my in-laws would be very unnerved if I gave birth to a boy who looked like Donny. I also knew that I wanted my in-laws to be involved in raising my child; it would be good for them, and they had done such an excellent job raising Donny. I read a lot of self-help books during this period—how to survive, how to make a better world. *The Road Less Traveled* was such an inspiration for me. I didn't go to any bereavement group; I couldn't take anybody else's grief. I know me: I would want to help the grieving person and that would just add to my grief. I tried to be stoic for everyone; I was afraid that otherwise we would all fall apart. I found support in being with people who had loved my husband, my two friends from childhood, my family and my especially close relationship with my Dad and my in-laws. Without my Dad's support, I would not have had the courage to survive Donnie's funeral and death. Walking into the funeral, my Dad called me "Jackie Kennedy" because of my composure. When I wasn't with my in-laws, my Dad was my rock.

Despite my grief, I survived and gave birth to a girl. When Donny was alive, we decided that if we had a daughter we would name her Dina. After Donny's death, I wanted to name her Donna but my mother-in-law disagreed; Dina was the name Donny and I had agreed to, and that's what she wanted it to remain. Dina looked exactly like Donny. The baby relieved some of my grief and brought joy to me and my in-laws. I was also grateful that when I went to the doctor in Colorado I was already pregnant because that meant I still had part of Donny with me.

I was never afraid of raising a child alone; I always thought I had enough sense to handle that. The thought of Dina growing up without a father didn't prey on my mind. How could I predict my child's future when I hadn't been able to predict my husband's death? I couldn't fix what had already happened to us but I could make Dina know that she was surrounded by people who adored her. And I was incredibly blessed with

Donny's parents being my in-laws. Interestingly, in spite of Donny's dying at 21, I never thought of my own mortality or its consequences for my daughter.

When Dina was almost two, I started cosmetology school. Although I received an allowance from the Army, it wasn't really sufficient. Without the benefit of a college education, going to cosmetology school was the best way to take care of our needs. The Army would pay for my schooling and give me a small stipend for expenses. My mother-in-law had already told me that she would take care of Dina for as long as it took me to get through school.

I started dating when Dina was about two and a half. My main concern was her well-being; even though she had only one parent, I wanted her to feel secure. In the beginning, dating felt awkward; it had been five years since I had first dated Donny. I didn't know how 23-year-olds were supposed to act when dating. I went out for several months with the first man I dated. Although his parents were crazy about Dina, he didn't want a woman with a child.

As always, my in-laws were supportive. They wanted me to be happy again, and they expected me to date and get remarried. They just wanted to be included in any future relationship I would have, and I absolutely wanted them included. I was dating but I wasn't actively pursuing either a boyfriend or a husband. Although I didn't have any fear of getting remarried, I didn't have any overwhelming desire to do so either.

I met Eugene, a musician, when friends and I went to hear a band in which he was playing. We got married when Dina was about four. My prerequisites were that I had to be sure that Eugene would not mistreat Dina in any way and that she would be comfortable with him and his large Italian family. I wanted my daughter to have a stepfather, a male figure, but only if he were the right person. I didn't feel any guilt about remarrying; Eugene loved children and I had such a deep connection to Donny that I talked to him and told him that Eugene would be good to Dina. After Eugene and I were married for a few years, we realized that we wanted another child. We went to Donny's parents and asked them if it would be all right if Eugene were to adopt Dina so that everyone in the family would have the same last name. My in-laws agreed, saying that they didn't want Dina to feel like an outsider. And to their credit, they always included Eugene and our second child in all their family activities.

Of course, I had concerns about Dina growing up without a father. When she was about two or three, I started introducing the concept of a father. I would show her pictures of Donny and say "Pop-Pop," and then, "this is your Da-Da." Because I had remarried when Dina was about four, she didn't really start asking many questions about where Donny was or what had happened to him until she was in her teens. It wasn't until she was about 14 that she learned the exact facts of his death — instead of believing he had been killed during the war.

I learned much from my experiences. Of course, I knew that Dina's welfare always came first, but I also realized that it's important to maintain a strong relationship with your in-laws: it is so important for your child to know where she came from. Your in-laws can impart so many more stories about her father than you can; she can learn so much about her legacy from them. I also learned that you cannot compare your second husband to your late husband; you can't and won't find a duplicate of your deceased husband. Each person has his pluses and minuses. When you find another person, make sure he loves your kids, and shares your morals and life-style — and love the traits and qualities in that person.

~ 12 ~

Benita Leitner — If You're Here, Give Me a Sign

*"Being Orthodox helped my grieving process. . . .
To honor Scott, I needed to be good and thankful for
all the blessings in my life, to go on for both of us
and live a happy and positive life."*

Benita Leitner, a Modern Orthodox Jewish woman, was suddenly widowed in 2000 at 47. She and her husband Scott, 49, had been living in their community in Pennsylvania for only three weeks when he died.

I met Scott on a paddleball court at a community pool in Brooklyn when I was 14 on the day I graduated from junior high school. He was extremely good-looking, and I thought he was snotty. All my girlfriends were crazy about him, but I was the one he liked. After I went out on a date with him to the movies, 14-year-old me told my friends I was going to marry him. I just knew. We dated for five years, and married in 1972 when he graduated from college with an engineering degree. He was 21, and I was 19. I had accumulated around three years' worth of college credits, but I quit when we got married.

Scott's first job required that we move to San Francisco in June 1973. In 1975, during the recession, we experienced "LIFO"—last in, first out—and Scott lost his job. He accepted a new position and we moved to Houston, where we lived for 23 years.

Scott and I were not Orthodox Jews when we married but we were always fairly observant. We belonged to a synagogue and went to services on Friday nights with our two children. In 1987 or 1988, after about 16 years in Houston, I found where I was meant to be religiously: Scott and I became Modern Orthodox Jews. Religiously, we were slowly moving to the right. We moved to downtown Houston and we went shul shopping, visiting all flavors of synagogues. When we came to the Orthodox synagogue, we both felt like we were coming home. It brought back all the feelings of my youth and my upbringing. We had always imparted to our children enough Judaism that we believed was appropriate for their age, so by the time we entered the Orthodox world our kids fit right in. They had gone to Jewish overnight camp, they knew the rituals. Now they also attended Jewish religious schools and spent time in Israel.

In 1998, we moved to Silver Spring, Maryland. We joined Young Israel, and religiously, this pulled us further to the right. Scott started wearing *tsitsit* (specially knotted ritual fringes or tassels attached to the four corners of the *tallit* (prayer shawl) and *tallit katan* (everyday undergarments). He put on *tefillin*— phylacteries, a set of small black leather boxes containing scrolls of parchment inscribed with verses from the Torah that are worn on the upper arm, hand, fingers and forehead during morning prayers. He also went to shul on the Sundays he didn't have to work.

After two years in Silver Spring, we again moved for business reasons to Elkins Park, a suburb of Philadelphia. Three weeks after we moved to Elkins Park, Scott was dead. He left for work on Friday morning, and two hours later, I received a call to go Abington Memorial Hospital. Scott had suffered a dissected aortic aneurysm. We were so new to the area that I didn't know where the hospital was or how to get there. On Sunday morning, a doctor with a perky smile on her face told me in a perky manner that, for all intents and purposes, Scott was brain dead, and that the diagnosis wouldn't be confirmed until Monday when the technicians came in. I was devastated by the diagnosis, but also was furious with the manner in which the doctor had delivered the news. To make matters even worse, my children were right there with me hearing this. It didn't matter that they were young adults—this was their beloved father. I asked her if she couldn't have found a nicer way of telling me. I remember saying, "Maybe I should call my mother-in-law and tell her not to come to see her son because ... for all intents and purposes he is dead— maybe she should just wait for the funeral information." I added, "You should never be in my shoes, but if you are, I hope some doctor treats you kinder than you just treated me."

Now I faced the difficult end-of-life decisions. I spoke with the rabbi of the Orthodox congregation in Elkins Park that we had just joined. He wanted me to digest the situation. The Wednesday after Scott had suffered the aneurysm, the rabbi said that the proper thing to do was to very slowly turn the respirator down. If Scott continued breathing on his own, then we should keep him on life support and do the best we could to bring him back. If, however, he could not breathe on his own when the respirator was shut down, we could talk, but he believed it would be all right to shut off the life support system. He told us that there were other rabbis who would never stop life support, but that the group of which he was a member believed it was religiously and morally proper to take a patient off life support if he could not breathe on his own. Scott's breathing was then tested, and he could not sustain breathing on his own. My mother-in-law and I could not watch them shut down the life support. I immediately turned to her and said that I had no regrets about the life Scott and I had shared together. Other than the usual silly arguments couples have, we had had a very loving and romantic life together. Yes, there had been some financial struggles, but our first, second and third priorities had always been the importance of our relationship with each other and our families.

Interestingly, Scott had once described to me an out of body experience he had when he was five and sick with croup. During the episode, he had seen doctors and nurses working on him and he described the tunnel and the light. He didn't like to talk about the experience as it gave him the willies. When he told me about the incident, it affected me. I came to feel that God had kept Scott alive for a reason, whether it was to bring children into the world or whatever. From then on, the thought was always at the back of my mind, though not Scott's, that he wouldn't have a long life.

Because I leaned on my Orthodox beliefs, I didn't get angry about Scott's death and never felt that it was meant as a punishment. Of course, I cried a lot and was sad that we wouldn't have a longer marriage and grow old together but I was never bitter. I was so grateful for what I had had; most women didn't have the kind of marriage I had with Scott. I know that my religion provided me with that feeling. I knew that although

Scott's physical life had ended, his spiritual one had not. After my grandmother died, I became active in a Jewish organization that, without ever uttering a word, silently washes and prepares bodies for burial (*tahara*), and Scott had also participated in this ritual. *Tahara* helped shaped my sense of what happens to a person once they die: the soul hovers over them until they are buried. But the soul never dies; the body goes away and becomes dust but the soul goes up to heaven and continues to live there, though we can't see or touch the person, which is painful to us. When Scott died, I felt as if he were still here with me.

Being Orthodox helped my grieving process. I felt that it would be an affront to who my husband had been if I were to become sour, bitter or angry. I believed that it would be a testament to who Scott had been if I were to live my life so as to make him proud of me. To honor Scott, I needed to be good and thankful for all the blessings in my life, to go on for both of us and live a happy and positive life.

I went to a couple of bereavement groups twice but walked out of each feeling depressed. People there had been going for years and just seemed to be pulling each other down; I felt the negativity, and realized it wasn't for me.

Of course I encountered problems. Even if you count your blessings, you still feel pain. Scott's death took a physical toll. I woke up two weeks after the funeral with two pinched nerves that sent me to the chiropractor for three months, plus the hair at the front of my head turned gray from ear to ear. And, living in a new place just three weeks before Scott died made life hard. I woke up each day and went to work as an administrator of a new Jewish school. I had no established friendships. My children were living in New York but I restricted my visits to them as I didn't want to encroach on their lives. Again, my religion comforted to me. Wherever we lived, we immediately became involved in the synagogue, helping out with whatever had to be done. Yes, every Orthodox community has its quirks but it will always help and support you. And mine did.

Sitting Shiva was very impactful. Although we had only lived in Silver Spring for two years, I was incredulous at the number of people who drove hours from our former synagogue in Maryland to Howard Beach, Queens, to pay their respects while we sat Shiva at the home of Scott's aunt. Similarly, the people in my shul in Elkins Park were very good to me. There I was, a newcomer all alone, and they would send food over, visit me and invite me for Shabbos meals.

Weekends were hard. I turned 48 right after Scott died. I felt young enough to be independent and take charge of my life. Although a lot of people invited me for Shabbos meals, the weekends were long and lonely if I didn't have an invitation. To pass the time, I read a lot of novels, and I went into my office on Sundays. About a year after Scott died, I decided to expand my life. I enjoyed outdoor activities, so I found a Jewish hiking group. It was a pleasant day of activity with a group of motley people with whom I knew I would not become friendly. Once I went on a Discovery Weekend that presented Judaism in a way that most people have never experienced it—a wonderful weekend comprised of all different varieties of Jews. I tried a Jewish singles weekend, but only once—it was filled with bitter divorcees. I did want a social life in addition to my religious life. Once I became friendly with women in the synagogue, they started throwing me together with men. I met one such man about 18 months after Scott died. I didn't start dating him immediately; we just went to Jewish functions together. It was nice to get dressed up, put on perfume and feel like a woman again. It developed into a compatible dating relationship. I missed not having someone to do things for, and I married him three years after Scott died. I never felt any guilt for remarrying. I never made comparisons between my new husband and Scott—I knew that it wasn't fair to make comparisons. But after three months of being married, I realized I had made a mistake but figured that God must have had a reason for the marriage. I stayed married for nine and a half years. The divorce became final in 2013, just after our tenth wedding anniversary. I've since remarried a Jewish man from a different background. It's a happy marriage but even if I tried I couldn't recreate my marriage to Scott. Again, it's not fair to make comparisons.

I should mention that many people do not realize that Judaism is a very mystical and spiritual religion. It is, and that has helped me. A few weeks after Scott died, I was standing in my apartment praying. The air conditioner wasn't on, nor was the fan. I put the prayer book down and spoke to Scott, saying, "If you're here, give me a sign." A couple minutes later, two or three of the vertical blinds began to shake. I have no explanation for it. I got shivers. Later on, when our daughter was having significant medical issues during her pregnancy, I felt Scott's warm breath on my face. It was a calming feeling. I told my daughter not to worry—everything would be fine, and it was. I definitely felt and feel that Scott is still with us.

I think it's worthwhile to remember that even if your life wasn't perfect, if you had a great marriage where you loved each other, had each other's back and put the other first, you're blessed to have had that—others don't. And, yes, it's hard to be a widow, but, widows shouldn't just babysit their grandchildren, complain and wallow in their widowhood—they should get a life. If your husband was a really wonderful man, believe he's still here and live the rest of your life to make him proud.

~ 13 ~

Rita B. — I Was Shocked ... Shocked That I Was No Longer a Mrs.

"After my husband's death, I had to transition quickly from being a child to a grownup....
I had now inherited many responsibilities."

Rita, a stunning business entrepreneur, 84, was 57 when her husband of 32 years died three months after having been diagnosed with cancer.

I was shocked when my husband died—shocked that I was no longer married, shocked that I was no longer a "Mrs." Our marriage had been a crazy relationship. Both of us were very neurotic. I had not had the happiest of childhoods. I had been emotionally and sexually abused as a child by my mother, and I spent my youth feeling sorry for myself. My marriage had been a repeat of my childhood, including emotional and physical abuse. I didn't have the confidence to get divorced, and it just wasn't done in my family. Consequently, I have spent most of my life in therapy or analysis.

I loved my husband but I had not taken my marriage all that seriously; it was a loosely knit marriage, and I had been unfaithful more than once during our marriage. Then a platonic relationship with a married friend developed into a sexual relationship and he became my soulmate, companion and best friend for the rest of my life. I do not believe my husband knew of my extramarital activities.

For the three months that my husband was sick, I worked from home in order to be with him. When he died, I grieved for my daughters—my married daughter who was about to give birth and my daughter who was in college—because they had lost their father. I didn't particularly grieve for my husband and it didn't particularly bother me that he wasn't going to live to enjoy his grandchild, as he never cared all that much for children or even for pregnant women. I did grieve in that I missed him; I grieved that I missed not being able to share things with him. I never felt guilty for my love affairs.

I started dating immediately after my husband's death. The weekend after his death, I travelled to New England to attend a symposium at his alma mater. I had always enjoyed going to these symposia with him, and I wanted to attend this particular one. I also thought going would be a good escape. I met a man there whom I then dated.

After my husband's death, I had to transition quickly from being a child to a grownup. I had been a career woman much of my life with household help, so I had had few domestic responsibilities. But I had now inherited many responsibilities. Being a focused person, I knew that I had to move ahead after my husband's death, and I also knew that I didn't want any one feeling sorry for me. Therapy helped. The first year after my husband's death, I didn't really feel anything because there was so much to learn about my husband's failing business. He had been neglectful of the family business. I had to take all the necessary steps to put his business affairs in order, including disposing of its assets. I also had to manage the distribution of his estate. It was hell. I had had no idea what was going on. I also had to learn who I was. In a way, I was lucky. At 57, I was young enough and had the energy to overcome new challenges: how to write a check, how to sell a business.

My husband and I had never had the usual couples-centered social life, so I never experienced couples dropping me from their social life. After his death, no one ever offered to introduce me to anyone. But I was always dating. No one scorned me for dating; honestly, I don't think anyone noticed.

During that first year I was so busy with the business and estate matters that I had no time for making new friends. But after the first year, I wanted to present myself as a new person. I wanted to let people know that I had my own life. I started making new friends. I invited people to dinner—not just couples, but also single men and women. I started hosting salons because I wanted to be around people I liked. When you invite people to your house, you're saying, "I'm me." If you were nothing before because you were a widow, you are now a "somebody."

After my husband's death, I learned many things about myself. I also learned that one shouldn't make any major decisions during that first year, whether it's where to live, to remarry or whatever. That first year, everything is a jumble; you're looking for a quick fix, something that's going to make you feel better—but it's not the time to make any such decisions.

~ 14 ~

Maria D. — The Cubbyholes of Life

"To help with the grieving process,
I came to visualize my life in cubbyholes.
Carlos' death was in one of the cubbyholes.
Sometimes it was as if I would take something out
of that cubbyhole, let myself think about it and cry,
and then I would put it back in."

Maria was 47 when her husband, Carlos, died a week before Christmas in 2003 of a rare bacterial disease, leaving her with two young sons. Although she never remarried, she was in a serious relationship for ten years with a man who died in September 2015 and considers herself a "double widow."

*C*arlos and I met when I was 17 and he was 16. We dated for seven years before getting married—I come from a very strict Latin background. My parents were born in Cuba and immigrated to the States in the early 1950s. Because my father didn't trust the intentions of any young man, I had to be chaperoned on all my dates. At first, my mother served as chaperone, then my younger sister, and later, married couples. We married in 1981 after we graduated from college. Birth protection failed and I became pregnant two months after we were married. Unfortunately, our baby died at birth. About ten years later, in 1992, our son Ramon was born and in 1996, our son Richard.

Carlos and I owned a transportation company with 40 trucks and over 60 employees, and we were both involved in the management of the company. Carlos was seriously injured in a near fatal race car crash in 1989, requiring extensive hospitalization and physical therapy, but other than that, he didn't have any medical problems. Then suddenly one Thursday night in December 2003, Carlos complained that he felt feverish and that his body ached. Although he felt under the weather, he went to work on Friday, but by Sunday he could barely walk. When we left for the hospital that night, he had to use a walker just to get to the car. On Monday afternoon, the doctors were able to identify the flesh-eating bacteria attacking his system. They administered the proper antibiotic but warned me that this disease was fatal 99 percent of the time. On Monday night, Carlos' heart stopped for the first time, but the doctors resuscitated him. His heart stopped again early Tuesday morning, and they resuscitated him, but the doctors weren't optimistic. Then his system shut down at noon and he was dead at 45. I was totally unprepared for his death. If anything, I had always feared that he would die from being overweight or from the stress he was under because of financial problems with the business.

Carlos was dead and there I was at 47 with our two sons. Ramon was eleven and had ADHD; Richard was seven and high-functioning on the autism spectrum. After my initial shock subsided, it was "tie the shoelaces on your sneakers and go" for me. I did my crying in the shower. I had to keep our trucking business going and for four months I did that, but then I realized that running the dwindling business wasn't for me. I sold off the remaining assets to pay business debts and closed the business. Fortunately, I did have insurance policy money for us to live on.

My first priority had always been my sons. Ramon took Carlos' death much harder than Richard. He was older and had a closer relationship with him. Unfortunately, when we were on the way to the hospital, Ramon had chided Carlos. "That's what happens when you go out without a jacket in the cold weather." The usually super calm Carlos shouted at him, "If you can't say anything good, don't say anything." That was the last time Ramon spoke with or saw his father and he never got over that exchange of words. During the 36 hours of Carlos' hospitalization it had not dawned on me that he was dying so I never took the boys to the hospital. Because I knew Ramon was having a hard time with his father's death, I took him see a psychologist several times. But Ramon didn't open up until four years later when I once again took him see a psychologist. That was when I learned that my outwardly happy-go-lucky Ramon was holding it in and was angry with me that I had not taken him to the hospital to see his father. I explained to him that it had never really been an option, that everything happened so fast and Carlos had looked so horrible and disfigured that I would not have wanted him seeing and remembering his father like that. He then understood. Richard was more accepting of Carlos' death.

Just as my boys have always been my first priority, they were also now my sole focus. I wasn't focused on my future, I wasn't looking for another relationship. My most intense pain and concern was focused on the reality that my boys didn't have a father. I was fully committed to dedicating myself to their future, and that was especially true of Richard, who might well always need some extra guidance and parental involvement. I was incredibly busy and was constantly on the go, whether it was driving from one kid's school to another, volunteering at school or whatever. But of course I experienced the loneliness and loss of companionship that are all part of the process of grieving. I would grab for the phone to call Carlos to ask him a question, but... To help with the grieving process, I came to visualize my life in cubbyholes. Carlos' death was in one of the cubbyholes. Sometimes it was as if I would take something out of that cubbyhole, let myself think about it and cry, and then I would put it back in.

I always tried to stay positive. My devotion to my boys, my family and my religious faith were my main sources of support. I read somewhere that, "There's a reason for everything that happens, and that reason is not necessarily for your benefit." Even immediately after Carlos' death, I believed exactly that. Importantly, this is where my faith kicks in. When I was outside Carlos' ICU hospital room and heard the Code Blue alert, I knew it was for him. I dropped to my knees, and prayed. "Please Lord, don't take him from me, but if you do, who am I to question?" I didn't know what Carlos or his future would be like if he had lived. Would he be a vegetable? I would end every prayer with "Lord, your will be done." Going to church served as an outlet for me: I would become emotional, express my sadness, cry and get some measure of comfort. Although I still went to church every Sunday, now I prayed more. Prayers, talking to God, my strong religious belief and knowing that God had my back helped me. I never once asked, "Why me? Why him?" I didn't question God, and I was never angry with God.

I never went to a bereavement group because I had started healing and I didn't think it would help; it would be like sticking a finger in a wound. About half a year after Carlos died, I did go to a psychologist for a few months. Even though I was handling things, I did feel overwhelmed and I didn't want to fall apart. I shared my fears with my psychologist and speaking with him gave me confidence. I stopped going when I felt more confident.

A new life gradually opened up to me. After Carlos died, I socialized mostly with the mothers of my son Ramon's friends, whom I had known since Ramon's pre-K days. Two of the mothers had been with me at the hospital all night and at the time of Carlos' death. The boys would be present and the social experience was focused on the children instead of the grownups. In March 2004, a few months after Carlos died, an usher in church introduced himself and expressed his condolences. From just chatting after church, a friendship gradually developed and we started dating a year and half later. Bob and I dated for about two years, but we waited four years after Carlos' death before making it official with my family. I had avoided any relationship because of my boys. Although initially it didn't sit well with my sons, they came around and developed a relationship with Bob. Starting the new relationship helped me tremendously; it made me feel good about myself and gave me confidence that I could still attract someone. More importantly, I had someone to share my life with again.

I was resolute that I didn't want to remarry. Out of respect for my boys, I wanted to be in control and make the decisions in our household. I also wanted to keep my financial assets separate with no commingling. Even though Bob and I spent all our waking hours together and considered ourselves married, I knew I wasn't going to marry Bob, so I wouldn't allow him to move in and sleep over at my house. For all the years we were together, until the last four months of his life, Bob went home each night to sleep.

Bob was three years younger than I. Several years after I met him, he became disabled. In 2007, he had an accident, severely injuring his ankle. He was a diabetic, and as a result of complications he was placed into a medically induced coma, during which time he suffered a heart attack, leaving him with a heart condition. He was in and out of hospitals after that, usually due to his diabetes. At the end of 2012, he was diagnosed with end stage renal disease and started on dialysis. I believed God put Bob in my path. I am a nurturer and I've always felt it was my mission in life to take care of others. Because he wasn't getting proper dialysis, toxins were building up in his body and he suffered a psychotic episode. He was hospitalized four different times. Because he was so sick, he moved in to my house beginning that May. In September, he passed out at home and I had to give him CPR. He died 12 hours later at 55.

Again, I was devastated. Although Bob had not been a healthy guy, I couldn't believe I had lost him so soon. I felt terrible for my sons as they had grown close to Bob. My father had also grown close to Bob, and that concerned me—since my mother had just died six months earlier, I was responsible for him. When Bob died, I considered myself a widow again. I loved both of them but differently. They were different relationships. Carlos and I grew into adulthood together; we were together for over 30 years, whereas Bob and I had been together for 10.

Once again my religious belief sustained me. I was comforted by the fact that I was able to take care of Bob during the last few years of his life, especially as he wasn't close with his family. While I don't necessarily believe that it is my destiny, perhaps my mission in life has been to take care of people.

Now my life revolves around my sons and my Dad. I drive Richard back and forth to college, a total of 92 miles daily. My circle of friends has dwindled and they're mostly couples. I don't have time or the desire to go to singles events. After Carlos died, I had not looked for a dating situation, and dating is not on my radar now. I don't know that I can handle a third relationship from a pain standpoint, which isn't to say that I wouldn't casually date again.

I would advise grieving widows not to be afraid to talk about your feelings—there is no shame in accepting help. For example, friends finished my Christmas shopping for me and wrapped the presents when Carlos died; an attorney friend helped make sense of my financial situation. Friends have always been there for me, and I have relied on the ever present love and support of my family. Remember that as long as one is alive, there is something to live for.

~ 15 ~

Rochelle Toner — I Was Scared That I'd Never Feel Joy Again

"I think the grieving process is probably the same for a homosexual couple as it is for a heterosexual one, but the grieving process might have been more difficult for me in a more restricted atmosphere, in a different geography, if I had been forced to live a more closeted life."

Rochelle ("Rockie") Toner is a lesbian, artist, retired faculty member and college dean. She was 62 when she lost her partner of 23 years, Almitra David, a poet and Spanish teacher, in 2003. Ms. Toner maintains a Day of the Dead memorial consisting of photographs and Mexican Day of the Dead artifacts in a corner of her living room, most of which were collected before Almitra died. To honor Almitra, Rockie asked that one of Almitra's poems be included at the end of her narrative.

We were both 40 when we met in 1981 at a women's weekend retreat in the Poconos. Although I didn't know Almitra, I agreed to attend her poetry reading with a friend. I harbored the fear that her poetry might not be very good, but in fact, I was impressed. After the reading, I introduced myself to Almitra and complimented her poetry. She asked me what I was doing that night and we clicked. We were never far apart from that day on.

I never married and had been openly gay for a long time. I was fortunate to be able to be out in my professional life: first as professor of printmaking and then as Dean at Temple University's Tyler School of Art. Almitra was married at the time we met and the mother of three children, 12, 14 and 16. For the sake of her children, Almitra was living together with her husband and kids in Kutztown, Pennsylvania. She and her husband had an agreement: they both saw other people—he dated women, she dated women. For several years, until her two oldest children were in college and the third a high school junior, Almitra divided her time between tending to the children at the family's home in Kutztown and then returning to her studio apartment in nearby Reading, Pennsylvania, where she taught English as a Second Language at Reading Area Community College. We alternated weekends in Berks County and Philadelphia. In 1985, Almitra decided she wanted a formal divorce and to be with me full-time in Philadelphia. After two years teaching in Temple's Academic Bridge Program, Almitra got a job teaching Spanish at Friends Select, a private Quaker school in Philadelphia.

Almitra had her first bout with breast cancer in 1985. It recurred in 2001 and although chemotherapy and radiation helped at first, the cancer metastasized throughout her body. She died 18 months later, in November 2003.

After Almitra's death, working in my studio was a sanctuary and an escape. On the advice of a friend, I went to a counselor for a few months. The counselor wanted to prescribe meds but backed off when I told her, "I'm not clinically depressed; I'm situationally depressed." I'm Irish and I had an alcoholic father. I was concerned that I might start drinking too much so I was very careful to limit myself to a drink or a couple of glasses of wine a day. I still have my two glasses of wine a day. After Almitra's death, I thought there would be stages of grief that I would pass through; that's what you hear, that's what you read. But for me it just didn't happen that way. If there were stages, they were so diffuse that one stage passed imperceptibly; I think I may still be going through these stages—it seems to me to be a life process. Although I didn't stay depressed and kept myself incredibly busy, I was scared I'd never feel joy again; then at some point, maybe three or four years later, I recognized that there had been a subtle change. It came as a reflection. "Wow, I really enjoyed that. I could get out of myself and enjoy things without thinking constantly, Boy, this would be so much fun if Almitra were here."

Almitra's kids were and are a source of support. We all worked hard on maintaining our relationship. The kids love me, the grandkids love me. They call me "Abu," short for "abuela," which means grandmother in Spanish and is very easy for an infant to say. I am very grateful for their presence in my life. I'm fortunate to have the kids, their families, an incredibly dependable and loving group of friends, and a wonderful sister.

When Almitra was dying, she bought me a gift certificate for a set of golf clubs because she said I would need something to do after she was gone—a wonderfully prescient present. I immediately got into golf and along with work in my studio created a path into my changed life. Although I had not felt a need to create a new circle of friends, golf exposed me to new people and became an important outlet for me. Our mutual friends were extremely supportive and are to this day. I never felt the tension that some people feel of not being part of a couple and so no longer a part of the group. Maybe the art world is more open—it's not such a coupled world. Just as I didn't intentionally look to meet new friends, I didn't look for or even think about romance. I had three kids, my Almitra family, and I think it would have been harder for me to stay as close to the kids if there had been a new person in my life. If romance had come along and found me, I wouldn't have rejected it—true emotion would probably have overridden concerns of family complications.

Dealing with the Commonwealth of Pennsylvania's tax laws was a major problem for me after Almitra's death. Because at that time we could not legally marry in Pennsylvania, I was subject to an inheritance tax on fifty percent of everything that Almitra and I held as joint tenants-in-common. It seemed incredible and completely unreasonable that after twenty-plus years together building a life I would be required to pay inheritance tax on the money and property that we had accumulated together. If we had been straight and married for five minutes, I would not have had to pay any inheritance tax. This is why the new laws have been so important for gay and lesbian couples—*fairness*. At a time when I was dealing with life-changing grief and loss, I was subjected to a very difficult tax burden. I am very grateful to everyone who worked to change these laws.

Mealtimes were one of the most difficult problems for me. Dinner was the hardest; it was the time when I felt the loneliest. Dinner is the time when couples come together and share the events of the day. We always cooked together, a simple dinner or a feast for the holidays—we loved the ritual of food.

Another problem that I still face is not having that special person in my life who thinks I'm fabulous. Almitra thought

I was brilliant, the funniest person she knew, and simply great. Everybody has some self-doubt, some vulnerability and everyone needs someone in their life who thinks they're the greatest—I still miss that. I also miss all that we shared together in the art world: the partnership of making work together, talking about art, going to openings and poetry readings.

I think the grieving process is probably the same for a homosexual couple as it is for a heterosexual one, but the grieving process might have been more difficult for me in a more restricted atmosphere, in a different geography, if I had been forced to live a more closeted life. I also think that the world is easier to manage as a couple: you can divide the responsibilities, you can bounce questions off someone you trust and, of course, you share expenses. You also share the fear of aging and its aches and pains.

If I have any insight, it is not to have any expectations of what or how you're going to feel or when you're going to stop feeling one way or the other; just be as positive as you can. Let life and death have its run. Let it be as it is. I love life and so did Almitra.

"After Reading Jung's Thoughts on the Afterlife"

Almitra Marino David (1941-2003)

we grow more contemplative
with age preparation
for life after time is
neither the tide nor the
beating of your heart nor
how a star moves slowly fast
through black yet
think of a thread of one that
sews a strange unity of dreams
so unshakable that even in sunlight
it holds together
and even in the dark.

~ 16 ~

Tammy Banks —
The Shape of Grief

"It wasn't until years later that I found out that Zeke had missed so many days of school not because he'd been sick but because he'd been frightened of coming home from school and finding me suddenly gone, just like his dad."

Tammy Banks, a writer, was 34 when her husband Tim, also 34, was killed in a car crash in 1995.

*A*s an engineer for G.E. Medical Systems, Tim was sometimes late coming home, but I had a bad feeling that July night. Because I had to stay home to put our three-year-old son, Zeke, to bed, I first asked a neighbor and then my in-laws to investigate the report of a car accident on a heavily rain-slicked road that Tim might have used to drive home. At first, there was no news. Then the police told them that Tim's van had crashed, killing him immediately. My in-laws came and broke the news to me.

At first, I felt as if somebody had cut off a limb. Throughout the first year, I was numb a good deal of the time. I was functional: having to care for my child took precedence. But I felt as if I were in limbo, a landscape where nothing grew. The numbness completely wore away during the second year. The pain hurt like hell, but it was better than the numbness.

I'd been raised Jewish, but I wasn't religious. I was at loose ends, trying to make sense of something that didn't make sense. I found a counselor who was into all sorts of different things, like past-life regression. I read and explored a lot of New Age offbeat stuff. After about a year, I stopped all of it as I decided I was getting too much into it and it was time for me to take my life back. I never tried conventional therapy or support groups. I've never been much of a group person.

For a while, I couldn't write. Then, inspired by my counselor's suggestion, I wrote an essay called "Letter to Tim" that I eventually entered into a writing contest. It won a prize. But I realized you don't really say goodbye. I also realized that I didn't believe in the five stages of grief. Grief is not that clear-cut; if it were, we would manage it better. I think grief is more circular, changing its shape. Periodically, you come around to the place where you were before—hopefully, you're a little stronger, a little better able to cope.

Tim's family and my own were very supportive. I also received tremendous support from an old family friend, who had been widowed in her early 40's, and from Tim's grandmother, whom I visited weekly. People can only follow you so far when you're dealing with your grief; sometimes all you need is someone sitting next to you without any need to talk. Some of our old friends were supportive in their own way and included Zeke and me in things; others just faded way. Actually, it was a pretty good litmus test: people showed their true colors. My cats were also a great source of comfort, just sitting there with me, providing unconditional love. (Animals never say things like "At least you had love in your life" or "This is my friend, Tammy. She's a widow.")

I felt very sorry for myself for a while after Tim died. I struggled with that as I knew it wasn't a healthy attitude. To ward off loneliness and to keep busy, I tried different activities, like horseback riding or Tai Chi.

Having to care for Zeke was the prime factor in helping me through the grieving process. What also helped was immersing myself in my writing. When I was writing my first novel, I would pour my loneliness into the heroine, who had also suffered a great loss.

Tim's untimely death created needs and consequences for Zeke: he needed to be close to me; he'd get nervous or angry if he couldn't find me right away, even if I were just outside chatting with a neighbor. It wasn't until years later that I found out that Zeke had missed so many days of school not because he'd been sick but because he'd been frightened of coming home from school and finding me suddenly gone, just like his dad.

Not having Tim to share things with still upsets me. Through the years, there have definitely been times that I resented not having him there him to talk important issues over with.

I started dating about four years after Tim's death. I knew that I was never going to find anyone like Tim. When I was younger, part of me thought it would be nice to get remarried so that Zeke would have a stepfather, but nobody was quite right for both of us. When I was in my early 40's, I decided I wasn't going to spend the rest of my life worrying about remarrying. If it were going to happen, I told myself, it would happen. I haven't dated in many years, but I feel the same way now. Yes, it would be nice to have someone to share things with, but it can't be just anybody.

Over time, I learned to say, "Widowhood is something that happened to me—it's not who I am." In our own ways, we all try to create new lives. It's hard. There's always part of you that wishes you could have your old life back. I learned that there was no such thing as closure, and I gradually learned to live with Tim's death. I think you have to let yourself feel the pain—stay with it for a while and let it wash over you. The only way out of the pain really is through it.

~ 17 ~

Patricia Goodman — The Terrible Problem of Loneliness

"His suicide was an escape from Alzheimer's and an act of compassion for us."

Patricia Goodman, a horsewoman, poet and singer, was 66 when her husband of 47 years committed suicide in 2007.

*D*ave liked to tell people that he knew he was going to marry me ever since the day he saw 14-year-old me do a face plant during a Handy Hunter horse show class. We started dating while I was in high school and Dave, eight years older, was in dental school. He worked his way through dental school by teaching three brothers to ride each weekend at the same stable at which I was taking lessons. We married in 1960 after I graduated from college. We were both horse crazy and except for our family, horses became our life. We bought 100 acres of land and had a horse farm in Chadds Ford, Pennsylvania that we ran for 40 years. At times, we had as many as 200 horses. We bred horses, we boarded them, we ran a riding school, and we even supplied summer camps with horses. All the while, Dave was a highly respected and dedicated orthodontist with a very successful practice in Wilmington, Delaware.

Dave's mother had died of Alzheimer's around 1986. That preyed on his mind very much and definitely influenced his actions. Dave was a person who was very much in control of himself and his behavior. He wasn't going to let uncontrolled circumstances dictate how was going to leave this world. For years he worried about having an exit strategy from his dental practice. In 2005, he had a small stroke that affected his ability with numbers; when using the phone, he would think one number and press another, and he couldn't balance his checkbook. One day in late 2006, he came home and announced he had to sell his practice. I don't know if the stroke caused or increased a fear of dementia, if he was having a series of small strokes or if he was experiencing the beginning of dementia—whatever it was, something seemed wrong. He began having difficulty sleeping. He became almost paranoid that he wasn't going to be able to sell the practice yet he kept trying to find a buyer. I think he knew his mind was beginning to fail and that he had a narrow window to take control of his actions and ensure that his affairs were in order.

I came home one day in late summer after doing errands; Dave's car was there, the house door was locked, the alarm was on, but there was no Dave. I searched for but couldn't find him, so I called our children. They drove all over the farm but couldn't find him. After coming back to the house, my daughter, a lawyer, found a note from Dave addressed to her. The note was a jumble, expressing his exasperation at not being able to do certain things anymore and mentioning details he wanted included in his obituary. Once we realized his intention, we resumed our search. My youngest son found Dave crumpled up next to the tree stand he used for hunting, dead from a gunshot wound. I had lived with the man for almost 50 years; the minute I saw him, I knew what had happened and why. I thought to myself, "That's okay—that's the way he wanted it." When I bent down and held him, I said, "It's okay, honey, it's over, your suffering is over. It's okay." I never felt any anger at Dave or personal guilt. I knew Dave just wasn't going to let that damned Alzheimer's take him out and cause us pain. His suicide was an escape from Alzheimer's and an act of compassion for us. I admire him; often I silently thank him when I see people struggling with Alzheimer's and women watching their husbands go through that awful disease. Dave didn't want to put us through that horror.

After Dave's death, I cried for six years. I didn't try to stop it. I just said to myself, Okay, you're grieving, you're going to cry and when you're done, you'll stop. And that's what gradually happened. I started to resurface. To be clear, it wasn't nonstop crying; it was intermittent and when I was by myself.

I briefly saw a therapist after Dave's death but didn't think it was very helpful. My four grown children were extraordinarily supportive: they took care of business and legal affairs, the physical demands of the farm and were there for me. I'm a poet; I didn't have a whole lot of friends, but my daughter somehow arranged for close enough acquaintances, including

Dave's aunt, to come over and keep me company every night for over a month. She even had a neighbor and former chef who had Parkinson's prepare and bring over ready-made meals. I am very proud of and grateful for my children's support.

Loneliness was a terrible problem. When Dave was alive, we did everything together. We had a very active social life and entertained like mad. At times, we had extravagant dinner parties twice a week, Fridays and Saturdays, with 12 to 14 guests. Dave's practice depended on referrals from dentists, so for the most part, these dinner guests were dentists, business acquaintances and only a very few were really friends. During the first few months after Dave's death, one couple reached out to include me and one other couple took me out to dinner once.

But I wrote voraciously—that's what really saved my life. My first book of poetry, *Closer to the Ground*, was published in 2014. Being able to write was my salvation. I didn't write much poetry while Dave was alive but his death created a reason for me to write more. A lot of grief went onto the page. A few weeks after Dave died, I went to a writing workshop at Osher Life Long Learning Center in Wilmington. I told the instructor about Dave's death and he told the class. After class, a woman I didn't know came up to me and said in a very warm way, "I'm so sorry. What happened?" Even though I hadn't really told anyone before, I told her. Betsy and I are now best friends. Me, who really didn't know how to have friends.

Dave and I had gotten out of the horse business. About 15 years later, I sold the farm and moved to a small community close to Wilmington and my daughter. The community was very small with no community activities. I started inviting neighbors to dinner, and I cooked gourmet meals, but I was a 70-year-old widow and they were all younger. What the heck do you do with a single older woman? I realized it was futile. I found a writing workshop in Rehoboth Beach, Delaware and a whole new world opened up to me. I discovered there was a large poetry community out there and in Wilmington. I am now very active and am in four different groups. I'm also teaching poetry workshops at Osher.

I am now a singer. I had studied voice in college but was too busy to pursue it while my family was growing up. At 77, I went with Betsy to hear the Osher Chorus and I joined it. Realizing I could use some help, I started taking voice lessons again. That year, music blossomed for me. I have raked this voice out of the gutter of disuse. I'm now doing solo performances as well as singing with the Osher Chorus.

In 2016, I moved to a retirement community with lots of social activities. I immediately got involved with its chapel sacred music services, not because I'm religious but because music moves me so. Interestingly, romances flourish in this community, even with men ten or more years older than me, but I have no interest. There is no way I'm signing up for that.

Looking back, I would say that a widow's job for the first year or so is to grieve. Don't let anybody tell you to keep a stiff upper lip, to get up, to get out, to get going and to get over it. Grieve. If you want to cry, cry. If you want to suck your thumb, suck your thumb. Grieve, but don't wallow. Everybody does it differently. It's a very individual and personal matter. And don't make any decisions that first year. You don't know in that initial time what you're going to want. Let it unfold. Also, be prepared: I have found over the years that there are times, for no apparent reason, that I am depressed and have crying jags. Then I realize that it's the month or the days leading up to the anniversary of Dave's death. Your body, your psyche, knows and will remember that time in your life.

~ 18 ~

Susan Gross — Finding My Spark

"You have to cry, scream, punch pillows—you have to let it out, or you will crash. You can't program every single day so you don't have a moment to think. I needed to lie in bed a long time before I found my spark but I did find it."

Susan Gross, a former schoolteacher, 74, founded the Philadelphia Chapter of The W Connection, a national organization that provides emotional support to widows as they deal with their grief and helps them establish a new life. She was married to Alan for 40 years when he died in 2003 after ten years of medical issues.

*M*istaking Alan for someone else, I approached him at a dance when I was 14. Although he was with a date, he asked for my phone number before he left. He called the next night to ask me out and we were an item ever after, except for a year break to he could sow some wild oats. I was 19 and a sophomore in college when we got married. Alan was 21 and had just finished his senior year in college. He had a friend stand in for him at graduation while we were off on our honeymoon.

After graduation, Alan first worked in banking, and then insurance. I taught school, which I loved. We had two children: a daughter, and a son, who has special needs and a wonderful loving heart and disposition. Alan realized he had a strong desire to pursue his artistic side and love of photography, especially capturing photographs of the sea. He left the insurance world and became successful selling his photographs and posters all over the world. Many medical institutions and doctors' offices bought his photographs because they had such a soothing effect.

Alan's business required that he exhibit at art shows. He had to frame 30 to 40 pieces, put them in boxes, load and unload the car with the heavy boxes, and set them up for each show. As a result, he developed back problems which were the start of his medical complications; over a 12 year period, his pain drove him to seek the help of many doctors. He underwent various new medical procedures, including insertion of a spinal stimulator, and then a morphine pump. He had to have back surgery when the catheter on the pump dislodged. Instead of helping Alan, all the procedures caused chronic pain, as scar tissue wrapped around his nerve endings. He reached a point where he couldn't walk and required a scooter to get around. Later, he was unable to work anymore and he lost his sense of self.

Finally, Alan had to go into a rehab nursing facility, and we were told they couldn't keep him there if he didn't make sufficient progress. He also had diabetes and edema, which could have affected his heart, and he ended up having a medical emergency at the facility that required taking him to a hospital. Everyone but me realized he was dying. I came to the hospital straight from a meeting with our son's new social workers, to tell Alan about all the good things that the new social workers expected to happen for Matthew. Five minutes later, Alan was on a respirator. I think that when Alan heard the good news about Matthew's future he was able to let go. Because the doctors didn't want Alan to suffer, they didn't want to take him off the respirator until he was in a drug induced deep sleep. The next morning, they took him off the respirator.

I was in a daze. Sitting Shiva was somewhat strengthening, with everyone making visits, but it's a false reality and then it's over. If people call a week later and you can't get out of bed, they'll never call again. For a long time I would walk around crying. If anyone, even a stranger, looked at me, I would say, "My husband died." School started in September and I had been assigned a different grade level to teach. I said, "I can do this," but I only lasted two weeks. I had no control over my emotions: I couldn't do lesson plans, I couldn't control a class. I went on sick leave and for a year, I went to a therapist. I didn't find it all that useful—it just felt like a crutch. My rabbi referred me to a bereavement group in the suburbs that was supposed to cure me at the end of seven weeks, but it didn't. I became friendly with some of members of the group and occasionally went out to dinner with them after the group ended. I suggested to the women that we set goals for ourselves, and they looked at me like I was nuts, so I stopped going.

That first year, while on sick leave, I did only what I had to— drive Matthew to work, buy food, and manage the household.

Other than that, I would lie in bed, read self-help books and listen to the Reverend T.D. Jakes and Joyce Meyer of Joyce Meyer Ministries. Other than my kids, those two were my support group. My friends didn't really get it and they couldn't fix it. People don't really want to hear—even now, people don't realize that Alan's death still hurts. I'll always remember Joyce Meyer's words. "If someone asks you how you are, say 'I'm struggling well, thank you.'" That should give people the idea that it isn't so easy.

I think the second year is harder than the first because reality sets in then and you have to deal with it. As I see it, during the first year, you're still trying to figure out how you could have changed the ending, plus you have financial and other matters to sort out. I pushed myself to do things during the first year but always gave the disclaimer, "If I start to cry, just ignore me." After a year on sick leave, I realized I couldn't handle teaching anymore and I retired in 2004. During the third year, I got involved in Hanna House, a halfway house for women. First, I knitted squares to be used in making afghans that were given to the women as rewards for self-development. Later, I became a board member and then president. I also urged my temple to host its own bereavement group, and they agreed as long as I would lead it. The temple advertised the group in its bulletin and a number of widows signed up. In 2010, one of our members saw an article in the *Huffington Post* about The W Connection, which isn't a bereavement group, but an organization that helps women build healthy and productive lives while they adapt to the new realities created by their husband's death. It provides widows with easily accessible emotional support, information and training. I went to New York City to meet the founders, Ellen Camp and Dawn Nargi, and then here in Philadelphia we started the first satellite chapter, with ten women attending on a regular basis. Now there are seven chapters and we're looking to grow. It's a wonderful feeling to see widows who had been strangers connecting with each other. To see a woman come to her first meeting crying and by her second meeting she is connecting with the other women, telling stories, laughing—that's pure gold. I employ many of the same techniques I used as a teacher to keep our Philadelphia chapter members engaged. Recently I requested that each member write a haiku about her grief and challenges, and we read them at a meeting. *The Philadelphia Inquirer* wrote an article about it. A local television station did a segment on one of our meetings, and another program just filmed an interview with some of our members.

I noticed that most of the women, regardless of how long they had been married, didn't have a sense of self. When you're married, it's easy to avoid things you're afraid of, and that's because your husband will do it for you. Your whole frame of reference is gone; you have to get your footing back. Being a widow either forces you to do things or it paralyses you. It's important to realize you're a widow but that's not all you are— you're also a person. When Alan died, I said, "I don't want to become bitter, nasty and paralyzed." My involvement with The W Connection has given me confidence and it has definitely improved my life. In helping widows establish a new life, I realize I was establishing a new life for myself as well.

Three years ago, I got involved in meditation, which has helped me a lot. I'm more confident and peaceful, and I've made amends with people who hurt me very much after Alan died. Even now, getting through some days can be hard but it's not awful. I just live in the moment.

My experience is that widows have to find something that sparks their individuality, the strength that they had, and build on it. You have to cry, scream, punch pillows—you have to let it out, or you will crash. You can't program every single day so you don't have a moment to think. I needed to lie in bed a long time before I found my spark but I did find it.

~ 19 ~

Debby G. —
Women Mourn, Men Replace

"We live in a couples' world, and that's the worst.
People forget about you; it doesn't mean they don't
like you, it's just that they forget about you."

Debby was 69 years old when her husband, 93, died in 2013. An attorney, she spent most of her career as a businesswoman in a successful family-owned business. She and her husband, Eddie, had been married for almost 24 years when he died.

*W*hen we married in 1989, we were almost 24 years apart —I was 45 and Eddie was 69. It was a second marriage for us both: my first marriage had ended in divorce and his first wife had died. I had worked for Eddie since 1974, but ours had been a strictly business relationship while his wife was alive. Eddie had been in excellent health and was extremely vital and physically active up until the last year or so of his life. He was also an extremely successful businessman, a major contributor to many philanthropic organizations and the arts, and a supporter and board member of numerous civic organizations. He was universally liked and respected in our community.

In 2012, Eddie underwent successful heart surgery. The only issue after the surgery was that he was unable to swallow properly and had to have a feeding tube inserted because he wasn't able to eat. During the following eight months of his physical decline, he was in and out of the hospital, rehabilitation and interrupted stays at home. He experienced several bouts of aspiration pneumonia, which ultimately was the cause of his death.

Despite his age, it wasn't until a couple of days before his death that we abandoned hope he would survive. But in those last two or three days, Eddie decided that enough was enough, claiming that he wasn't going to fight to live any longer or try anything new to extend his life. It was very hard for me to accept that, but I had to do what he wanted, to respect his wishes, and stop urging him to fight.

Eddie spent the last two days of his life at a beautiful hospice. I wasn't there when he died. The hospice nurse said that patients often died when the family wasn't present; it was as if the deceased wanted it that way. His last words to me were, "I have no regrets, I had a great run."

It was hard for me to accept that this very vital person was no longer with me, although the grieving process had started during his decline. I was sad and mournful, and I missed his companionship. Despite his age, I felt that I had not had him long enough. I had been single for 17 years between my divorce and marriage to Eddie. In some ways, I felt the mourning more intensely and I was more bereft after my divorce in 1972 than I was after Eddie's death. I wasn't as confident a person back then as I was at the time of Eddie's death, and I wasn't as prepared to carry on. Although Eddie's death was painful, I knew that I could get through it. I did go to a support group for a short period of time, but I had become more cognizant of my own emotional strength. I knew I could learn from bad circumstances; I knew that people respected me for myself and not just because of Eddie's prominence, and I was able to move forward and be okay. I should add that I think the Jewish process of mourning, the ritual of sitting Shiva, is very psychologically healthy and comforting to the bereaved.

I noticed that as Eddie got older he became much more concerned and protective of his biological family's financial well-being. He transferred the bulk of his assets, including the family business, to his children over the last 15 or so years of his life, yet he remained concerned about their financial well-being after his passing. At the same time, he seemed to be less and less concerned about my ability to have a financially secure future. He expressed his confidence that I would have no difficulties after he was gone, despite the fact that his earnings accounted for the vast majority of our combined income. I don't know if this is typical in a second marriage situation or specific to our situation. This caused a strain in our relationship and in my relationship with his family, but fortunately, the strain passed and I have maintained good relationships with his daughters, their respective spouses and children.

For the first year or more after Eddie died, I was very concerned about whether I would have sufficient income to maintain the life-style we had shared. My problem was exacerbated by the fact that Eddie had paid many of our bills directly from his accounts at the office, and I didn't really have a handle on what our expenses were, as I never saw the bills. I had always maintained my own checking account, and paid many of our bills from my account, but I didn't have an overall picture of annual expenses. Immediately after he passed away, I set up a projected budget on my computer and have continued to faithfully enter all expenditures. Though I was quite shocked to learn how much I needed to spend annually, I have since become comfortable knowing that I can maintain my life-style, and that barring stock market disasters, I should be fine going forward. Having said that, I still find it very useful to keep track of all my expenditures, and it's a practice I would highly recommend to anyone, and particularly to widows who didn't manage the family funds before their widowhood. It's also very helpful when dealing with accountants and financial planners.

Another major problem I encountered after Eddie's death was realizing that we live in a couple's world, and that's the worst. People forget about you; it doesn't mean they don't like you, it's just that they forget about you. I decided to counteract that by entertaining at home. I invited a mixture of people, both single and married, for dinner. It helped me a lot. I put together a group of people who now owed me invitations (although the number of invitations I received fell short of the number I extended). I realized that my happiness depends totally on me. For various periods of my life, I had been very much a loner, but now I value the company of people in my life much more. Eddie and I had been very much involved in the cultural and civic activities of our community, including attending the Philharmonic and the theater. I decided to continue that involvement and have renewed our two ticket subscriptions so that I can invite people to go with me. I didn't hide behind a tree: I volunteered to help people in our congregation by cooking in the synagogue's kitchen; I joined a book club, and I signed up for adult education classes. I would be interested in dating, though I'm not up to meeting someone online or sure about how to go about meeting men.

Within three or four months after Eddie passed away, I realized I had to go on with my life. I am more serene now and more comfortable with myself, realizing that although it may not be pretty, life does go on. While I am very busy on a daily basis, I still feel lonely at times, and sorely miss Eddie's companionship.

I find this an interesting observation: my brother's wife passed away about two years ago. She had suffered from Parkinson's disease for almost a decade and he had taken very good care of her. Within a few months of her passing, though, he had a girlfriend, and they have been together for about a year. I have to say I'm a little bit jealous. But one of my widow friends made the following observation. Widows mourn, men replace.

~ 20 ~

Sandy M. —
The Long, Winding
Process of Grief

"I thought grief was something I could work through, like a college class. And, if I worked hard enough, maybe I could get over the grief before the baby came. Now I realize that grief is a long, winding process and we have minimal control over how quickly we process and heal."

In July 2012, Sandy, an East Coast native, 32, was living overseas and three months pregnant when her husband, Ted, 32, died suddenly.

*W*e met at a summer series basketball game in high school when we were both 15. By our senior year we had become good friends; we were the last to know that our relationship had turned romantic. Ted was different than the other boys I had dated — smart, thoughtful, artistic and athletic. I was hooked. We went to different colleges, dating long-distance most of that time, and moved in together shortly after graduation. I will always have fond memories of our years together in Washington, D.C. — getting our first jobs, finding our social scene. Ted was even in a rock band. In 2008, Ted's company offered him a position in East Africa and off we went, also getting married that same year. Life was exciting, filled with travel and adventure.

In 2012, everything changed. Ted had planned a few days trip to do some work and creative writing at a coastal resort that we used to frequent. I remember he was feeling restless and said he needed to get out of the house. He was bothered by some recent changes with his job, by the isolation of working from home, and by an injury from a recent motorcycle accident. He felt stuck and he had to get out. I stayed home from this trip, as I was three and a half months pregnant, and we had agreed I shouldn't take very many flights so early in my pregnancy.

Ted would be away from Wednesday morning to Saturday afternoon, and I would pick him up at the airport Saturday around 1:00 P.M. so we could have brunch with a friend. That Saturday morning at 7:00 A.M., I received a phone call from a good friend who was vacationing at the same resort with her family. She had forgotten her phone at a party at Ted's cabin the night before and when she went to retrieve it, she found Ted on the floor — he was dead.

The coroner shared that Ted's heart was very large and looked as if it had been working too hard for a very long

149

time—heart failure. His death certificate stated that the cause of death was cardiac arrest due to coronary heart disease. While understandable, given his many health concerns, this is not the full story, and I want to share it so that others can learn from our mistakes and so that I can heal.

Looking back, Ted had so many things going on at this time. In the months before his death, he was stressed by work and was not sleeping well. He would drink to relax and help him sleep and he would drink more on weekends. This escapism wasn't new: even when we were teenagers he always seemed to be trying to escape something, trying to walk that line. I always figured we would grow out of our bar hopping days when our baby was born because we would have new priorities. Ted had also been on a number of medications prescribed by his therapist for his ADHD, anxiety, and sleeping troubles. And in the weeks before, Ted had been in a serious motorcycle accident, nearly breaking his leg. Months earlier, we had also received warnings from our doctor in the States during our checkups that his health was in danger. She had warned us that if we didn't get Ted's weight under control, adding exercise and healthy eating into his daily routine, that there could be dire consequences. This was something we were working on improving, but being the young invincible people we were, crossing the globe at a moment's notice, we didn't give this warning the consideration it deserved. I remember during one of our visits she mentioned the possible onset of Type 2 diabetes if he didn't totally turn his health around, but it's all a blur to me. Why didn't we listen? Why didn't we make these important changes? Things were moving so fast back then. But I think the key factor was the death of Ted's mother and aunt just months earlier: this weighed on his mind, and he was never really the same after losing them.

I found out something that I wasn't expecting, though I'm not completely surprised by it: Ted had purchased heroin the night he died. He had told his friend it was "white crest," a kind of heroin thought to be more pure. He asked his friend to tell me not to worry, saying that it wasn't about me. I think maybe he knew I would blame myself. I know deep down it wasn't my fault, that so many things in life are out of our control, but I wish I had done things differently in our life together. I wish I had been more watchful, I wish I had nagged him more. I still sometimes wonder if his death was intentional. Was he trying to escape or was it an accident? I'll never know for sure. It's taken me years to share this with anyone. I was so scared that people would judge him for the choices he made. I was scared that because of how he died, people wouldn't be able to appreciate the amazing person Ted was or the incredible work he was doing. I was scared our daughter would feel abandoned, as I first did. The truth is this: I understand now that underneath Ted's brilliant and often lively exterior, he was really troubled and sad, and the decisions he was making in the months and days before his death likely made sense to him.

I was lucky that I had the support of good friends when Ted first died. They came to help comfort me and to deal with the police, coroner's office and local government bureaucracy to get his body released and transported. They also kept watch over me that first week, bringing food and making sure I ate, managing the calls and visits. My parents came to be with me and help settle my affairs. Ted's father and brother also made the journey, representing his family for the local services. Four weeks later, I was home in the States and starting the adjustment to what felt like a completely different life.

It took months to realize I was in shock those first few months and up to a year. I was like a zombie going through the motions each day—waking up, breathing, eating, and attempting regular interactions with other people. I remember a moment in the first week when I was sitting on our sofa: I realized that this was not a dream, he wasn't coming back and I was going to be a single mother now. I was stunned that life wasn't going to be as I had planned. Because of the baby on the way, I tried to focus on moving on. It wasn't until a year later that I realized that I had been so numb. Maybe that was my way of protecting myself; I was in shock, numb, fuzzy, sad, and angry—the moods didn't always proceed in a straight line. Sometimes things just hit me. I would move forward, and then feel angry, then happy, then some other feeling. It was like being on a roller coaster of feelings. I've come to realize that I'm never just going to get over it; it will always be part of me, who I am and what I'm thinking. Luckily, in more recent months and years, the pain has transformed into an awareness and an appreciation for life. Losing him made me reflect on life, what it means for me and what I want out of it both for myself and my daughter. Grief has the power to change people in big ways.

Anger for me was an emotion that came later and continues to visit me on occasion, but with less and less intensity as time has gone on. I was angry that things were not going to turn out the way I had planned or chosen. I had chosen to be with Ted, I had chosen to become a mother—we were going to be a family. Even though I've processed that Ted wasn't in a good place emotionally and didn't necessarily have control over his actions, I was still angry at him for leaving and sometimes even now I'm angry about the choices he made. Ted and I had our baby and so many other good things to look forward to and it hurt to think that he chose not to be part of that. I still struggle with these thoughts. I've also been angry at myself for not recognizing that he was so sad, so far gone. I remember our anniversary dinner two weeks before he died, when Ted said, "You and the baby would be so much better off without me." At the time, I had no idea what he was talking about and I told him he was crazy to think that way. I've been angry with myself for not recognizing the depth of his depression. I was angry that Ted had not had the happiest of childhoods. I was angry at Ted's company for not providing the healthiest of work environments. I've been angry with pretty much anyone and everyone at some point in time since his death. At four and a half years out, I'm starting to find some peace in forgiveness and in understanding that things happen that are simply beyond our control.

I was fortunate in terms of support. I had my family and Ted's family, and I had friends. I had the support of my therapist who I worked with for three years following Ted's death. I deliberately decided not to try a bereavement group as a means of support, having heard that the experience might be different for young widows. I also read as much as I could on the subject. But mostly I relied on individual therapy as a way to heal. I had so many questions about what I was going through and about my feelings and reactions. I've never been one to show a lot of emotion and I worried that I wasn't being a good widow, that I wasn't grieving him enough or missing him enough because I wasn't crying enough the way I had seen widows like my grandmother or widows on TV do. It wasn't until much later that I realized I was likely protecting myself. After all, I had a child to prepare for—I couldn't be lying in bed all day crying. I had things to do. I learned that there is no right way to grieve— everyone does it in their own way. For me, the tears came at night when all was quiet and I was alone, and I allowed them. These days I don't cry so much; it's just on occasion that something will remind me of him and I'll feel like crying. Luckily, I am also blessed with happy thoughts and memories that come to mind now—many more happy ones than sad ones.

My close friends back home were supportive. I could tell they felt for me and cared a great deal. Back then they must have wondered how they could help me, but I had no idea what to ask for and wasn't used to asking for help. Sometimes when we would go out, I would feel like I wasn't supposed to be there. It felt strange doing normal things like going to dinner or having fun when Ted was dead and not able to do those things. I felt like I didn't belong. It was painful to realize that now that he was gone, I might not maintain some of the friendships we had as a couple. It was also painful knowing I would need to navigate life as a single person in a very coupled-up world after having the security of a serious relationship for so long. But navigating social situations is getting easier as I become more confident in myself with my new life and identity.

After Ted's death, I was confused about who I was and what my life was supposed to look like without him in it. I had to figure out how I would fill the huge hole that his death had left. I had to work through the grieving process so I would be ready to be a normal mother, a good mother. I felt immense pressure to process Ted's death and to get comfortable with it so I could be that good mother. I didn't know about grief; I thought it was something I could work through, like a college class. And if I worked hard enough, maybe I could get over the grief before the baby came. Now I realize that grief is a long, winding process and we have minimal control over how quickly we process and heal.

A big portion of my grieving process has been related to protecting Ted's image so that the nature of his death doesn't adversely affect our daughter. I'm still processing this. It is only in this telling of my story that I'm beginning to have the strength to address this issue in my life and what a burden it has been. When Ted first died, I didn't think I could handle the stigma of how he died on top of the loss I was suffering. I couldn't handle the judgment, but now I'm more comfortable with the truth. More attention needs to be paid to mental health and substance abuse issues. Sometimes I wonder if our family and friends had questions surrounding his death. At times I felt that maybe they knew what had happened, but given all we'd been through, they didn't want to upset me so they didn't push or pry. Maybe they sensed it was too painful for me. I appreciate their love, respect and patience as I continue to navigate this.

When my daughter was three, she asked where her father was, and I told her he was in heaven. A couple weeks later, she asked why he was there and I told her it was because his heart had stopped working. I plan to share more when she's old enough to understand. I have told her all the good things about her father. Sometimes she'll talk about him on a daily basis, or ask a lot of questions about people who have gone to heaven. Sometimes she looks at me with this sweet, sad face and says she misses him, and it breaks my heart. I listen to her, and then tell her that some people don't live as long as we want them to and that her father loves her very much. I remind her that she has two loving grandfathers and uncles. She has asked me, "You're going to be here for a long time, right?" I told her yes, that that is my plan. Then I tell her that most people live for a very long time. I deal with it as best I can. She likes to stay close to me, and I try to be mindful of that. I think I can say that I'm less scared of death because I've been around it so much. But I do take a safer, less risky approach to life now. I want to be around for a long time because I want to be here for her, for all the positive things in my life, and for the things we'll do together.

I've been building a new life with new direction, new priorities. I like who I am and I'm embracing the changes that this tragedy created in me. I like being able to focus on my daughter and her early years. I'm also studying to get a Master's in counseling. If Ted is looking down on me, I think he'd be so happy that our daughter and I are happy together. Every few months, I have these moments when I realize I'm taking steps forward, moving on, and the tears are bittersweet; although I loved what Ted and I had together, from the sweetest parts to the messiest parts, I'm looking forward to the future.

I've learned a lot in the last few years. I've learned that I should try not to worry so much about what other people think—not about what they think about your grieving process, whether you should be dating now, or whether you should be acting a certain way. Learn to accept help from your friends and family. At first you may not know how or what to ask for but don't be afraid to ask for or accept help. And take the time to care for and be good to yourself. Things will never be the same, but they can get better.

~ 21 ~

Nora H. — The Caregiver

"He had been sick for 33 years and his death was a relief... I never went through a period of sadness or grief... I loved Tod very much but the years he had been ill had also taken a toll on me."

Nora was widowed in 2010 after caring for her husband, Tod, who had Parkinson's disease for 33 years.

I met Tod, a brilliant Ph.D. economist and university professor, in grad school, and we married in 1965 when I was 22 and he was 27.

In 1977 when he was 39, Tod was diagnosed with early onset Parkinson's. It manifested via a cramp in his left foot, and then his left leg. His condition worsened and walking became a problem. Often I drove him to work, as he reveled in teaching, which he continued to do until 1996.

In 1992, I started noticing some changes in Tod's behavior. The type of Parkinson's that he had comes with some dementia, and a medication he was taking, Mirapex, is known to cause compulsive behavior. In his case, it was gambling. To support the gambling, Tod was stealing money from our joint account as well as diverting money intended for our children's college fund. He knew what he was doing was wrong but his medication was in control of his behavior. I had to take steps to protect our finances, and he understood.

In 1996, Tod retired from academia and went on disability, and for the next ten years he remained at home. He could be functional or in a fog: it depended on where he was in his medication cycle, or on how much medication was in his system.

Around 1998, Tod started experiencing Sundowning and sometimes I would have to be up with him all hours of the night. He would do all sorts of weird things—he might leave the house in the middle of the night and go next door to a neighbor's. I had to start locking the doors. He became incontinent, and would black out from low blood pressure and fall down the stairs. He also started having seizures due to epilepsy. I took him to the hospital for tests. When he tried to remove electrodes that had been attached for a test, they put him in restraints. The hospital mismanaged just about everything they could, and I had to deal with their incompetence along with managing our household, our finances and the lives of other close family members.

I realized that it was time for Tod to go to a nursing home, and he remained there until he died in 2010. He had his good and not so good days. Even after more than 30 years of Parkinson's, there were days he could still remember people's names, watch sports events on TV, or engage in conversation and repartee. There was still a person in there. Other times, the nurses would have to yell at him to sit down as he tried to run down the hall. Although he might remember names or watch a ball game, I couldn't have a real intellectual conversation with him.

The day he died was one of his good days. He had walked to the dining room, eaten dinner, and come back to the nurses' station to kid around with them. But he died suddenly while sitting in a lounge chair. I don't know the exact cause of his death—I think it may be been related to his medicine.

Tod's illness was physically and emotionally exhausting. Another close family member also had medical issues. Attending the ballet and concerts had become my means of coping throughout these illnesses. I learned of Tod's death when I arrived home after an evening concert. I was calm. He had been sick for 33 years and his death was a relief. I never went through a period of sadness or grief. I hadn't been in a marriage; I had literally been on my own and a full-time caregiver for so many years. The things that we had liked to do— go to restaurants, travel, sit and talk about books or have an intellectual conversation—hadn't existed for so many years now. I loved Tod very much but the years he had been ill had also taken a toll on me. My life improved both physically and emotionally after Tod's death.

Although I experienced a sense of relief, I'm sure there are other women who react differently and for whom I am very sorry; some women go into a sort of collapse because their whole life had revolved only around their husbands. Although I had been Tod's caregiver for all those years, I was fortunate in that I did have other things, such as the ballet, concerts and my community work, that were essential and kept me going both during Tod's illness and after his death.

~ 22 ~

Samisa S. — A Guiding Spirit

"...right after my husband's death, I didn't believe in God anymore. I didn't want to have anything to do with Him. But now I understand that things happen for a reason."

Samisa was born in Calcutta, India in 1958. Her husband, Harsha, also a native of Calcutta, died in 1997 of a massive heart attack when he was 50, leaving Samisa with three young children.

*M*y husband, Harsha, and I met by accident in 1977, while I was vacationing with my family during Christmas in Chunar, a resort town in India. He was already living and going to college in the United States when he came home to vacation with his family in Chunar. The way I met him was very weird. While we were in Chunar, an acquaintance of Harsha's made a crude remark directed at me and I told the guy off. The guy was so incensed that he came to our vacation home the next day to try to get the last word and to complain to my parents about my comments. Harsha, who had not been present the previous day, was with him. Again I told that guy off, and apparently, my candor struck a spark with Harsha, who returned later to apologize for his acquaintance's rude behavior. I accepted his apology. After that, Harsha and I ran into each other a few times in town and would greet each other. As fate would have it, we encountered each other again on the day my family was leaving Chunar to return to Calcutta. Harsha spent some time talking with my parents and me, and we learned more about him. The conversation ended but we exchanged addresses.

I didn't hear from Harsha for a year and didn't think much about it. To my surprise, I received a Christmas card from him that Christmas. My brother and I wrote him to thank him, but my correspondence with Harsha didn't stop there. For a year, we wrote to each other across continents. Letters turned into phone calls once or twice a month, and a budding romance grew. I came to love him because I was impressed by how caring and loving he was and with his good morals. I liked that he respected my parents and that even during those expensive phone calls he would take the time to speak with them. He had asked me once if I was interested in coming to the U.S., and I answered yes. Little did I know that the question was a bit of a test, one that I guess I passed; he wanted to know if I was up for the adventure of a life with him.

Fifteen months after sending me the Christmas card, he sent me another card, a beautiful one that contained a marriage proposal. Once Harsha knew that I felt the same way about him, he sent a more formal letter to my parents asking for their permission for my hand in marriage. My father was enthusiastic about the engagement, but my mother was very worried—who was this man who was going to take her daughter so far away? Meanwhile, both sets of parents got to know each other in India, while an uncle, who lived in New Jersey, connected with Harsha back in the States. He got to know him very well and gave his approval, sealing the deal with my parents.

We got married in India in December 1980. After I finished college the next September, I joined him. I was 22 when I walked off the plane at JFK Airport in New York City, excited for my new life with my new husband in a new country. I wasn't at all scared. My husband had a good job and had settled with some of his siblings on the East Coast. I spent the next few years getting acclimated to life in America, being a wife, making a home, beginning my career, spending time with his family and traveling with him. We decided to start a family—our daughter was born in 1985. She was the apple of her father's eye and watching him with her made me fall in love with him even more. Four years later, we decided to have another child and learned that we were to have twins—our boys were born in 1990. My mother had moved here a few months before to help with the new babies. A month after the twins were born, we bought a house and spent the next few years raising the children, traveling and having fun together. During this time, my husband also encouraged my father and brother to move to the U.S. He wanted to make sure the kids, who already had his family here, were also connected to mine. My brother got married and moved out of state, a few hours away, to start his family. When his daughter was born, my parents moved in with him. Although there was a large Hindu community where we lived, we spent a majority of our time with family and close friends.

One morning in 1997 my husband called me at work. He was in a lot of pain, which he thought was heartburn. He decided to leave work and go home early. I called the doctor and made an appointment for later that afternoon. When I arrived home to take him to the doctor, he was lying on the couch as if napping, but he was black and blue. I realized he was unconscious and called 911. The dispatcher told me to move him to the floor and begin CPR—he wasn't breathing. I gave him CPR until the paramedics and police arrived. While the paramedics were in the living room trying to save my husband's life, the police were in the kitchen questioning me. Then they rushed him to the hospital while I stood outside the home we built together, completely in shock. Neighbors drove me to the hospital. There wasn't any good news when I arrived. "I'm so sorry, we tried our best but your husband passed away," said a doctor as I entered the ER. I stood there in utter shock—it was unbelievable. My neighbors were in complete shock, too. I didn't know what to ask, what to say, what to do. I still don't remember the details. At some point, the doctor said I could go see him. I walked into the room where he was and gave him a hug. I said I would take good care of the kids and then I left—still in shock. I came out into the hallway and called both our families. I called my brother first. I told him what happened and he said he was leaving right away to come be with me. My parents were on vacation in India. Then I called my husband's eldest brother, who lived close to us. My teenage nephew picked up the phone and told me how to reach my brother-in-law, but I don't remember speaking to him. I know my brother started calling people and letting them know because all I could think about was my kids.

I wanted to go home to meet my daughter as she got off the school bus, but she was already home. When I arrived, she sensed something was wrong. I felt like a robot explaining it to her. I didn't cry—I hadn't actually cried since I heard the news. She sobbed and then I began to cry as I consoled her, but I was also thinking about the boys. I needed to pick them up from school but I also needed to make the house look normal first. I sent my daughter upstairs while I cleaned the living room. It was in disarray after the paramedics had left and I didn't want the boys or my daughter to see anything that would scare them—syringes, medical wrappers, etc. My daughter went with me to pick up the boys. I was numb driving to their school. I picked up the twins, drove back home and on the same couch where their father had died, I told the boys of his death. Actually, I think my daughter told them—I still can't remember. The boys were six and had no clue what death was. It would take a while for them to understand it meant that he wasn't coming back. The twins started playing with toys as six-year-olds would and family began to arrive to be there for us.

Then I called my husband's office and told them he had died; they were also in shock because they had seen him that morning.

During the period following Harsha's death, we all reacted differently even though I tried to follow the children's normal routine when they were around. Me? I couldn't bear the sound of a siren, be it an ambulance, police car or fire truck. I had to stick my fingers in my ears. I tried reading some books on death, but mostly I just concentrated on the kids. When they went to bed, I would just cry. My daughter was very angry that her father had died. "He was a good person, why did he have to die?" The boys didn't cry much, but they had some temper tantrums; maybe that was how they were dealing with their father's death. At this point, we went to a professional counselor but it wasn't very helpful. I don't think we were ready to talk about his death.

It should be noted that everybody grieves differently, but everyone needs support. I was fortunate in all the support I received from both my husband's family and mine. For about a year, my parents split their time between living with my brother out-of-state and living with us, surrounding the children and me with love. Although I will forever be grateful for their love and support, sometimes I felt their presence was overbearing and I needed some space to come to terms with all that had happened, to be on my own, to understand who I was and how I was going to deal with things.

It took about a month for the shock to wear off. This was around the time everyone else went back to their normal lives and I felt alone. That's when I went through the stages of grief: I was angry, upset, confused, and restless—why had this happened to me? To him? To our family? I was trying to find answers, looking for signs. My daughter was still waking up in the middle of the night with nightmares. She had dreams about her father, but he never came to me in my dreams.

Six or seven months after my husband died, a friend wanted to introduce me to her guru, a Hindu religious teacher and spiritual guide. He lived in Chicago where Hindus from around the country could connect with him. I was skeptical of reaching out to him because he was celibate, had never married and I couldn't imagine he knew anything about true love. He didn't even have a family or know where he came from because he was an orphan. So how could he connect with me? But my mother encouraged me to talk with him. She said he could give me some insight and maybe help bring balance in all the chaos. She was right, of course. I was brought up as a Hindu, but I was never very religious. Before my husband's death, I practiced some of the Hindu rituals my mother had ingrained in me—like leaving an offering and water on the religious altar in my house. But now, I wanted nothing to do with God. I was very angry. I had believed in Him and He had betrayed me. But meeting the guru was a turning point for me. The guru became my spiritual guide, even coming to my home to be with me and my family. I was honored to receive a special mantra prayer from him. The mantra, or chant, was supposed help me concentrate in times of turmoil, so I could meditate and find balance. He told me that when-ever I had the time, I should just recite my mantra, and it would help strengthen me and help me cope. At that point, I thought, "Okay, I'll try it, why not?" Speaking with my guru and reciting my mantra gave me a different perspective, including on my husband's death. The guru showed me that death is part of life and that we have to accept it and move on, to find our inner strength.

Very importantly, I now truly believe that someone is there to take care of me, of us, when horrible things happen. As I've mentioned, right after my husband's death, I didn't believe in God anymore. I didn't want to have anything to do with Him. But now I understand that things happen for a reason, just like the guru coming into my life. He was there to be a change agent, and he showed me a path that drove me to be a different person. Because of what I learned from him, I came to realize that God is still there with me. He is giving me the strength to deal with the daily struggles in my life, to overcome them and He won't give me more than I can handle. I came to accept my husband's death. I have also learned that the best and most significant thing one can accomplish is to live a good life with integrity and make a difference in someone else's life. I've taught my children to live a good, honest life with decency and virtue. I am grateful to my guru, my family and friends and to the won-derful people who have come into my life, who always guide me to become a better person.

I've also learned new things about myself that I didn't know before. I've learned to be independent. When I was married, my husband often drove everywhere and I was content being a passenger. It's similar to how we were in life; we did every-thing together as a family, and I never imagined having to do this alone. I've also learned of my inner strength so I can make decisions based on practical things rather than emotions. Bad things happen in life and I cannot crumble when they happen. I have to get things done and be strong, so I can be a great mother to my kids. I know now bad things happen to everyone and I have to find a way to deal with it and move on. I know that I'm not alone in my pain because other widows are also experiencing their pain.

Becoming a widow comes with other issues. Sometimes, well-meaning but thoughtless people will say inappropriate or hurtful things to you. In my case, people unnecessarily advised me to take care of my children—like I didn't know that—and asked me if I was going to be able to manage without a husband. People asked my children questions at my husband's funeral that they should never have asked. All I remember about my husband's funeral, when I was still in shock, is a man I barely knew asking if I needed money. Some people will make you feel as if your life is over or ruined because your husband died. How will you survive in this world? That latter group wasn't there to help; it was sort of like they wanted to see me fail. Maybe they just didn't know what to say. Regardless of their intent, their words pinched at my heart. I separated myself from these people over the years.

I never wanted to date or remarry as I didn't want to risk exposing my children to a problematic stepfather. I immersed myself in my children's activities, becoming a soccer mom and volunteering at my kids' schools. Now the children are grown and living independent lives. I live by myself, but I don't feel lonely at all. My life is filled with activities, and I pursue my interests, continuing to learn about and practice spirituality, read good books, do volunteer work and finding nurturing and fulfilling pursuits. I realize now too that I never needed to promise my husband anything after his death. I could and did raise those kids well on my own and I'm proud of who they've become.

When you're grieving, that's all you think about, but don't give up—it all works out in the end. Stay positive. There's somebody taking care of you. It doesn't have to be God; it can be someone here on earth or an angel or the spirit of your lost loved one. They are guiding you always, just have faith.

~ 23 ~

Liz R. — A Pretty Tough Lady

"Grieve? I had no time to grieve; I had no time to breathe. I had to be able to emotionally and financially support my family."

Liz, a mother of two, was 55 when her husband of 25 years committed suicide in 2002.

y husband was a financial advisor and insurance agent, but he had made many foolish personal investments over the years that had a negative impact on our family's financial health. I was never allowed to be involved in financial matters or decisions. Also, my husband had a history of depression that had started in his childhood and continued throughout his life.

Around 2000, my husband became enamored with one particular stock in which he invested all our family resources. He refused to sell any shares, as he believed the stock was going to make us rich. At the time, we had a son in college who had been born with a heart defect and a daughter, a senior in high school, who was applying to colleges. Then 9/11 happened and the stock market plummeted, including the worth of the stock that was going to make us rich. Shortly thereafter, the stock's earnings report was released and the stock price sunk even lower, at which point he sold the stock and we lost our shirts.

Earlier in our marriage, my husband had been hospitalized for depression because of an unsuccessful investment. After he left the hospital, he seemed fine but was a different person. He didn't continue to receive psychological help. A psychologist friend who had been present at Thanksgiving dinner in 2001 mentioned to me that she thought he needed psychological help. Then one day I found him reading the Bible, which was not something he was wont to do. He said he was trying to find some comfort. He was very non-functional and depressed, and so I checked him in to the local hospital in early December. He admitted he was very depressed, had a gun and was suicidal. After he was released from the hospital, he entered a clinic that treats depression, and was there for two weeks before being released; he was deemed not suicidal. On his release, the clinic should have provided counseling to our family. Living with him was awful: we were always watching what we said, and were on pins and needles. The kids knew of his suicidal tendencies, but the world thought he was fine.

One day in 2002, our son was home from college for an athletic competition. I heard banging in my husband's office, and asked what it was, but was told it was nothing. My husband said he didn't want to go with me to our son's game. I went alone, and when I returned home, I didn't see my husband. My daughter, who was just leaving the house, said she hadn't seen him. I continued looking for him and calling his name but couldn't find him. I went out to the store to get a couple items for dinner but still couldn't find him when I returned. Then I opened the door to his office and found him hanging from the ceiling with a bag over his head—quite dead. My husband had been an Eagle Scout so he sure knew how to tie a knot! He had known what he was doing. He hung there for two hours until the coroner came. The police questioned everyone who had gathered in the house to make sure there had been no foul play. I was shaking—we all fell apart. We were so distraught: I couldn't go into the room—it was a nightmare. He had left no note nor did he leave any message on his computer. My son said that he had always expected him to do this. My husband, who always prided himself on planning everything, hadn't planned out who was going to find him hanging from the beams of his office. His daughter almost did. She had almost opened his office door before she left earlier that afternoon, but fortunately, she had not.

The nightmare continued. It took a long time for the shock to wear off. I was overwhelmed, and my daughter was distraught and hysterical. She felt her father's suicide made her stand out like a sore thumb at school and the school offered little support. Also, she had not received early acceptance at her preferred college. My son, away in college with a heart defect, was binge drinking. Grieve? I had no time to grieve; I had no time to breathe. I had to be able to emotionally and financially support my family. I was in crisis mode, and couldn't make time for personal therapy. This "man with a plan"—his investments hadn't gone as planned. At the time of his suicide, our financial position was terrible. The life insurance policy that my husband, the life insurance advisor, had left wasn't going to be sufficient to pay for college and support our family. I had to immediately figure out our finances—how we were going to live, how to pay for college, what to do with my husband's business and clients. I decided to take over my husband's business. I had to quickly become an expert on the business and save and service his clients' needs. The business demands were overwhelming. Ironically, three days before my husband's suicide, I was notified that I had passed the qualifying exam for the form of life insurance I now specialize in. Again, I had no time to mourn. I had to keep going, and I wasn't going to let my children down—they came first. They were going to get beyond this, they were going to be okay, and once they were okay, I would be okay. I really did make a go of the business and supported my children.

That first year was very hard. I had to make very difficult decisions by myself. It was excruciating. I was very angry at my husband, and I'm still very angry. Leaving the house was an enormous and monstrous experience—even going to the supermarket and walking down the aisles, thinking, "I don't have to buy the Wheat Chex or half and half anymore." People were repeatedly asking, "How are you doing? How are the children doing?" You knew they meant well, but you wanted to scream, "How the hell do you think I'm doing?" I couldn't sleep in my bedroom until I bought a new bed, and I could not step into my husband's office until it had been redone. I couldn't go into it at night for many years because I would see the image of the man I had been married to for almost 25 years hanging from the beam in the ceiling. Most people don't remember what was said during the funeral services, but I remember the rabbi invoking depression in relation to Peter Bogdonavitch's movie *The Mask*. Once you put that mask on, you become a different person and you can't take off the mask. Most people don't understand mental illness: there's a stigma to suicide. I also noticed that I lost friends; even my best friend wasn't my best friend anymore. Some friends dropped me because I was no longer a couple. I wanted company but it didn't happen. I would have paid for my own dinner but it's as if they were uncomfortable with the single me.

The second year was tougher emotionally than the first. The first year, I focused on surviving: I had something to prove. As for emotional support, I didn't have time that first year for any therapy and I didn't receive any emotional or financial support from my family. Some of my family members still chide me about a few of the funeral details. I got my emotional support from those friends who stayed true to me. One non-Jewish friend even went to synagogue with me that first Friday night. The second year was excruciating, as reality set in, and I realized that no white knight in shining armor was coming to save me. It was all up to me. I started grieving, and I wanted to be alone a lot. Although I wanted company, I sort of didn't want to have a social life; I didn't think I would be good company. I started missing my husband, and I gave in to moping. I would go to the cemetery, talk to my husband, yell at him, yell at his parents. I didn't forgive him, and I don't think I'm capable of forgiving him. During the second year, I had to come to grips with the fact that he had committed suicide, that he was sick. I was grieving, and I went into therapy. I didn't want to go to a support group and share my experiences with other people or listen to their experiences. A support group was not the right venue for me. I went to a couple of different psychiatrists, and the meds helped somewhat.

Then last year I tried mindfulness training—it helped. Only recently have I entertained thoughts about a new life. I don't date because I can't take rejection. I'm not good at losing clients. And a spouse's suicide is the ultimate "eff you." I don't want to create a new or expanded circle of friends, and I don't entertain. I do go out to cultural events, either with a friend or by myself. My husband had been very controlling, and I can't take that anymore. I find it much more complicated to have to deal with another person than to simply do something on my own, to do what I want to do when I want to do it. And, yes, sometimes I would like to have a man's perspective on things or invite a male acquaintance to a wedding. It's very awkward to go to a wedding by oneself, especially when all the couples are out on the dance floor.

I've learned a lot since my husband's death. During the first few years, besides figuring out how to secure my family and finances, I learned I had to take baby steps. I had to develop confidence; I couldn't listen to everybody, I had to listen to myself. I learned that I'm a pretty tough lady. I'm okay today. I've done well, I'm a good person, I help people. I've met people I would not otherwise have met. I've learned that as dark as a day or as insurmountable as a problem may seem, this too shall pass. Take a breath and go on.

~ 24 ~

Wendy M. —
A Dream of Polished Bronze

"Seeing David in that dream changed things for me.... After the dream, I did start dating and didn't feel guilty about dating. I had felt numb for so long; I wanted to feel alive again. I knew it's what David would have wanted."

Wendy, a human resources executive, had been married for more than 28 years to David, a university athletic director. He had always been a strong, muscular man until he suffered a brain tumor. Wendy was 53 when David died unexpectedly from complications following surgery.

*W*hen David was 42, he started having severe headaches. Eventually he was diagnosed as having a benign brain tumor. Because of its location and the state of the surgical technique, doctors thought that surgical removal of the tumor might affect David's heartbeat and breathing. So his neurologist thought it best to treat the tumor with radiation and chemotherapy, as if it were a malignant tumor, and to insert a shunt to alleviate David's headaches. He also had semiannual MRIs and checkups.

For ten years, all went well. David had no more headaches and was able to work full-time. Over time, I noticed that David had trouble with balance and that his speech had thickened. His former neurologist had retired and his new neurologist recommended monitoring David's condition for six months. During that period, his balance worsened, and I believe he was becoming depressed because of the changes in his condition and medical regimen. Because significant advances in surgery had been realized since his initial diagnosis, his new physician thought that his tumor could now be safely removed surgically, and we agreed to the operation.

The doctor said that David's surgery had gone well, and the growth that had been affecting his movement and speech had been removed. No further radiation or chemotherapy would be necessary. We were warned that because of the bleeding that typically occurs during brain surgery, blood clots could accumulate but precautions were being taken to prevent them.

After the operation, David was taken to a rehabilitation center to restore his speech, motor skills and functions. He had been in rehabilitation for two days when I received a 6:00 A.M. telephone call from the center telling me that he had been moved to a local hospital, and that I should rush over there. Although I didn't know it then, David was dead by the time I arrived at the hospital. A blood clot in his leg had traveled to his lungs. I waited by myself in a room until a doctor and priest came in. I immediately realized that David had died and I collapsed. My world was shattered. The doctor and priest had to climb under the table to get me.

I had to pull myself together. I wanted to be strong for my stepson and my daughter, who was going back to college in a month to start her sophomore year. After the initial shock, as friends and family started coming to the house, I was calm, I was numb, I was in control. I said all the right things, I did all the right things. I stood in the kitchen for hours, talking to people as if nothing had happened. Again, I just became numb, and I stayed numb for a couple years.

I did various things to keep myself occupied. I kept myself busy by helping my daughter stay focused on college. I believe her passion for dancing helped her through the shock of her father's death. She had started taking dance lessons when she was three years old and was very devoted to her dancing activities in college. After she returned to college, I would drive four hours each way to visit her in Virginia. This was the first time in my life that I lived alone and it was hard. I was very involved and active in my AME church: I headed up the women's ministry and I planned retreats and breakfasts. I read a lot of work-related materials to keep myself professionally current. I also got a little dog, a Bichon, who became my focus.

At night I would break down crying—nighttime was the worst. During the first two years, I put myself in a cocoon. I would go to work, come home, and eat a potpie. I don't know what it is about a potpie but that's all I would eat. I would listen to my telephone messages but I didn't have the strength to return calls. I would turn on the TV to watch the news. People would call and want to talk, to know how I was doing, but I didn't want to talk. All my strength went into getting through the day in a way that looked like I was in control. I had to insulate myself so that I could put on my "everything is okay" mask the next day.

I didn't go to a therapist because I didn't want to talk to people. There was a grief share group at another church, but that wasn't for me. I couldn't talk the way the other participants did and I didn't want to listen. I thought my situation was different. My hopes had been so high and then they dropped so low. David shouldn't have died, he should have lived and been home with me. Life had disappointed me — oh yes, I was angry at God. I was born in the church; my father was a pastor. I was such a good person who always tried to do the right thing and who treated people properly. All my life I had behaved that way, so I couldn't accept that this happening to me. But I got over that.

I didn't tell other people, but in my mind, I would talk to God. I'd say, "Just let me see David, just let me talk to him, just let me hear his voice." I believe God heard my prayers, and that He knew the only way I would get focused on living again would be for me to see and hear David again. One night I went to sleep and had the best dream I've ever had. At least, I think it was a dream. That night, David came to me, and it was the most beautiful thing. He didn't have a shirt on and he looked very muscular. His right shoulder was tanned — it was bronzed. I said, "David, you look great, you got all your muscles back." He said, "Yeah, I had to leave you, Wendy, because God had a job for me to do. I didn't want to leave you but you have to do what God wants." He told me that his right shoulder looked like it was polished bronze because of "...where I have to stand. It's the closest part of my body to God." I said I understood. That was what worked for me. After that, I said, "It's all right, I can go on."

Seeing David in that dream changed things for me. I sometimes ask myself what would have happened to me if I hadn't seen David in that dream. Before the dream, I wasn't even thinking about dating. After the dream, I started dating and didn't feel guilty about it. I had felt numb for so long, and I just wanted to feel alive again. I knew it's what David would have wanted. He would have wanted me to have companionship. When you're not a couple, everything changes. For a while, my brother and his wife shepherded me while other friends—ones who cared about me—just went on with their lives. You know, they're the couples. It was awkward for me, being the third. If I was invited to a party, I'd wonder if it was worth going and just sitting there by myself. I was fortunate, though; I didn't get around to creating a new circle of friends because I soon met a man through work whom I dated for the next five years. We both grew up with the same conservative background. I was sure we were going to get married and I was upset when we broke up. Since then, I have dated other men and am currently in a relationship with a wonderful man, an attorney, who I met by chance when I stopped at a hotdog stand to buy lunch.

One thing I do know: your grief is unique to you—there is no right or wrong way to grieve.

~ 25 ~

Linda M. — It Will Get Easier

"After Matt died, I was angry at God for a long time. I felt like I was the first single parent that this had happened to. Why had this happened to me?"

Linda was 35 when Matt, her husband and father of their three-year-old son, Jay, burned to death in 2001 because of a malfunction in his delivery truck.

I met Matt through one of my sisters and we were married in 1995 when I was 29. We were total opposites: I was raised in the suburbs and had lived a sheltered life with a homebody attitude, while Matt was more street savvy and hung out more.

I was totally devastated in 1996 when I gave birth to a stillborn daughter. Because of that trauma and subsequent miscarriages, I didn't tell people I was pregnant with Jay until about my sixth month. I was obsessed with my son, an almost crazy obsession. My mother admonished me that I shouldn't love anyone more than life or God.

Matt was a nighttime delivery driver in New Jersey for an international donut company. I came home one night to find one of my sisters crying. She had just received a call from our cousin, who had heard about Matt being in a horrible accident. Just as she started to tell me, the company called me and the police were at the door to tell me that Matt's truck had gone off the road, crashed into the side of a tree and burst into flames. The New Jersey State Troopers and people who recognized Matt from his route tried to get Matt out of truck, but they were unsuccessful and he burned to death in the cab. When the police came to tell me, I just passed out from shock and woke up in the hospital. Because Matt's body was burned beyond identification and his dental records had been destroyed in a flood years before, it was two weeks before the coroner would release his body. My brother-in-law went to the morgue to identify the body; the family wanted me to remember Matt as he was when he was alive rather than carry in my head the image of his charred remains.

An investigation revealed that the accident was entirely the result of a malfunction in the design and manufacture of the truck. Matt was entirely blameless. Although the accident happened at night, Matt had not fallen asleep at the wheel and not been under the influence of anything. His system was clean. It was extremely important to me and my mother-in-law that Matt wasn't in any way responsible for the accident, and that there was no evidence of any drugs in his system. Before I knew Matt, he had been incarcerated for selling drugs, so knowing that he was clean would help clear his name of any gossip. And he was clean. We were successful in suing and recovering damages from the manufacturer but what mattered most was that Matt was totally blameless.

After Matt's death, I was really scared about raising my son by myself. I was obsessively overprotective. At one point soon after his death, I simply told Jay that his father wasn't coming home again, and that he was in heaven. It was just the two of us from then on, taking care of each other. I'm not sure he understood, but after that day, he changed. The little boy was gone, and he had become a little man, a little man who didn't cry. He's always been very observant. While he was in preschool, he started drawing pictures of trucks on fire. It was hard on his teachers to see these disturbing photos, and it was hard on me. At one point, I did take Jay to see a psychiatrist but he didn't talk about his feelings about father's death or why he didn't cry. I sometimes think he didn't cry because I cried so much in front of him. Despite Matt's death, our relationship didn't change. We kept pretty much to our same routine. Because Matt had worked nights, Jay and I had the same evening time together as before. Jay wasn't clingy, and he didn't show any fear that something bad would happen to me. He had always been a thoughtful child, and I think he had come to the conclusion not to say anything, not to cry, not to immediately react. I did seek professional counsel but even now, Jay thinks about things before he reacts. He still holds things in. I think my son had a normal childhood, but as he got older, I felt confused; I felt I had to talk to someone about what kind of person I should be—just his mother, or his mother and father? Was I doing all I could be doing? No matter what I was going through, he and

I were fortunate that we always had family support. I'm very proud of Jay; he was accepted to every college he applied to and has successfully completed his freshman year.

After Matt died, I was angry at God for a long time. I felt like I was the first single parent that this had happened to. Why had this happened to me? I didn't ask for this, to raise a child, a boy, an Afro-American boy, by myself. I was depressed. My family tried everything to get me out of my depression, but it lasted a long time. I was on Zoloft for about two years. After Matt's death, I went for psychiatric counseling for about six or seven months but I couldn't connect with my psychiatrist. She gave me good advice but I wasn't ready for what she wanted me to hear. Because she wasn't agreeing with me, I thought she was against me. I went to a bereavement group, but I was still in an angry stage and didn't want to hear about and cry over someone else's loss. I just wanted to cry over my own. I had my own routine for dealing with my grief. I would come home from work, do homework with Jay, cook his dinner and put him to bed. Then I would go to my room, stay there and eat ice cream, despite my sister warning me to stop because I was hurting myself. Every time I heard the words "buy one, get one free," I was at the store buying ice cream, and that went on for quite a time. What snapped me out of it? About a year after Matt died, I took Jay and my niece to Disney World. I was shocked when I saw the pictures of me. I didn't recognize me, and I didn't look happy. I hadn't realized how much weight I had gained from my daily diet of ice cream, how I had let myself go as long as my son was happy. I can't overemphasize how those pictures catapulted me out of my depression. I started taking care of myself, I banned ice cream, and I went to Weight Watchers. I watched what I ate, I exercised, and lost 80 pounds — 18 in one week.

I was not only very angry when Matt died, I was very scared. We had planned our life together, and now I was solely responsible for raising my son. I had to learn how to be a single parent. I had been working as a temp, but after Matt died I got a permanent job. I still didn't have any health benefits for my son, but I learned how to sign Jay up for the CHIP program. It was perfect for him as he got health benefits that I couldn't otherwise afford and I didn't have to pay for it. I also had to learn how to let people into my life. I never liked asking people for help but I had to learn how—not for me but for my son.

The Baptist Church really helped me through the grieving process. I had been raised as a Methodist, but as an adult, I joined the Baptist Church. It got me to focus on the more positive things in life and made it easier to live with Matt's death. It helped me get over my anger and it helped me to grow. I became more humble, caring and understanding. One of the pastors who knew my story reached out to me; she insisted that I read some Scriptures. She understood why I was angry at God but explained to me that none of us is put here for a fixed amount of time; we don't know when, but we're all designed to leave this world at some time. She helped me understand that God had no intention of hurting me personally with Matt's death. God could have taken Matt at a time when he was still selling or taking drugs but he didn't because God knew that wasn't the life Matt was meant to have. God had helped Matt get clean. Two years later, at the time of his death, Matt was still going to meetings and staying clean. It could have gone the other way; he could have died while he was still doing drugs. And if he had died while he was still doing drugs, he would have been blamed for the accident, and the manufacturing malfunction would never have been discovered. No one else but God could have done that. I became further humbled when my son joined the Boy Scouts. I saw that there were people who were worse off than me. I saw that God had no intention of hurting me personally; he just showed me why he needed to take my husband.

Losing the weight gave me confidence in myself. I started taking care of myself, pampering myself, getting out of the house, hanging out with my girlfriends. I had to learn how to be sociable, how to let people into my life. Two or so years after

Matt died, I started making changes in the house. I repainted, I got new bedroom furniture, and redecorated the room where I spent most of my time so that it felt like mine. I also started reflecting on what I really wanted. I decided I wanted to date. I tried online dating and I met someone I dated for four years. I only dated people who I felt would be long-term. I wouldn't let just any man meet my son — only men I had been dating for at least six months.

I strongly believe you go have to go through several stages of grieving or you may find yourself going backwards later in life. I know I went through anger, depression, confusion and questioning as to how I was going to get through it. The grieving process can take years, but you have to totally grieve to get it out and get through it.

I must say that it really annoyed me when people would say, "I know how you feel." No, you don't know how I feel, you never even asked me how I feel. Each loss is different. I would say, "Thank you, but you don't know how I feel." I didn't say it in a nasty way because I realized some people just didn't know what to say or weren't thinking, but, no, you can't say that to me.

If I have any advice for grieving widows, it is this: If you're angry, stay angry. If you want to cry, cry. If you want to be by yourself, be by yourself. Don't hold back your feelings. Go through whatever you're going through until you're over it. But keep your energy positive while you're grieving. Remember that every day you'll meet people who have it worse than you. Believe in something while you're grieving; believe in God, or a person who has been good to you — it makes it easier. It will get easier! And don't just live for your children, live for yourself too. Also remember to keep all of your memories alive — good, bad, whatever.

ACKNOWLEDGMENTS

I cannot sufficiently thank the "wonder women" in this book for their generosity in sharing their lives, experiences and innermost feelings with me, with us. I am especially grateful for the trust and confidence these women, women I had not previously known, had in me that I would relate their personal stories accurately and in their voice. I hope I have validated that trust. I hope they know that the kindness of their openness will be of help to many women who are anxiously confronting widowhood. My thanks also to the widows who were similarly generous in recounting their experiences even though the book does not contain their personal stories.

Being a neophyte author, I have been fortunate to have been able to pick the brains of and draw upon the wisdom of good friends, Paul Dry and Franklin "Buck" Rodgers, experienced publishers, who generously provided me their time and knowledge, and the highly regarded author, Dan Rottenberg. Thank you for helping to educate me and for your patience. A very special thanks to my most wonderful friend, the extremely talented and accomplished graphic artist, Toby Schmidt Meyer, herself a widow, for graciously insisting that she would be delighted to create this book's wonderful front cover and design.

I would be remiss if I were not to express my thanks to all of my wonderful friends for their encouragement and patience. I am also very appreciative of all the kind friends and new acquaintances I met through networking and social media who took the time and made the effort to introduce me to widows they thought would be interested in sharing their personal stories and experiences.

And a very special acknowledgment to the two most important people in my life – my sons, my heroes. Thank you, Jamie, for your encouragement and confidence in me; thank you, Tom, for both your valuable advice and substantial expenditure of time and efforts on my behalf. And, thank both of you for weathering my journey through widowhood with me. A mother could not have better sons. Your father would be most proud of both of you!

CPSIA information can be obtained
at www.ICGtesting.com
Printed in the USA
LVHW040809190819
628118LV00019B/914/P

9 781545 661062